DEDICATED TO MY SWEET MOTHER JANE GRAHAM BERTUCCI, AS I WILL DEDICATE EACH AND EVERY BOOK I WRITE TO HER. SHE WAS MY REASON FOR LIVING, AND FOR HER ETERNAL MEMORY, I CONTINUE ON THROUGH LIFE WITHOUT HER. SHE GAVE ME MY SENSE OF EQUALITY AND A TRUE PURPOSE FOR LIVING. I MISS YOU MA.

1

Voting for Fun and Rebellion

How to feel confident and powerful while voting with a different way of thinking.

We belong to a group of people who are very tired of the same old results from the same old voters. This Voting Bitchfest will specify criticism of the way we are forced to vote. Please. We are not that stupid, and political crap does not easily sway most of us. We want to be having a blast pissing rich and powerful people off and helping humanity at the same time. Let's get together and make this one big voting party and speak louder than the rest!

Chapter 1
Apparently, voters are worthless

First of all, do you think your vote matters at all? Currently, not voting makes more sense to those who want citizen's ideas and hopes to fail. You realize that if money has not changed hands, the voting means nothing to the most greedy and corrupt of people who run for office. You see, our voting methods and results are existing in a greed-based world. If there is no money exchanged for votes, it would seem that the people elected may have a problem on their hands as to how to generate votes.

It also appears that our generations have started to be complacent about voting and having their voices heard. What the heck is up with that? How come we haven't been so excited and thrilled to participate in the process in which we are all governed for well over 200 years? Why is it we cannot seem to get out of the house, office, school, or work location to execute a very simple task? I have a feeling it has something to do with the actual process itself. People have a fear of the Voter's Information Book as well as the fear of doing the wrong thing. The responsibility seems too much for most, so it slows down.

Somehow we have all been inundated by the voting methods involved in the process. For the younger folks, the voting process seems daunting. Throughout the years, I have noticed the voting informational "pamphlets" are filled with confusing contradictions, wording that makes no sense, and candidates who are vague in their positions.

I can't blame anyone who doesn't want to fool around with a process that makes them feel like they are back in school, taunted by the school teacher or Proctor of a test. Man, those people make me nervous and to walk into a polling place with the scrutiny of the old codgers behind the registration desks, etc., well, that just makes me freak out totally.

Somewhere along the line there must be a better way to do this without making it seem like a trip to the Dentist, or a relative's house for dinner. Somehow we have to make this a process that takes a little time, the issues are laid out in a simple fashion, and the confidence in doing the task is confident. The confidence and sureness of the voting act are the secrets to walking into a polling booth and knowing for a fact your needs met. The confidence in understanding the things you are voting on, people you are voting for, and the effect of your vote on others will be to everyone's advantage. The way you, as a voter, can be a part of the positive change in a population of people should make you feel wonderful! The problem is, for most who participate, the feeling is sad and unfulfilling.

I had hoped to make the voting process fun, exciting, learned, and perpetuate people's position in our society as revered. People can look up to a kind hearted and patient person while understanding that all humans should be considerate of others. People can treasure the people before them who have assisted in giving freedoms, rights, and humanity back to the people of our country. These are the people not concerned with how the environment is undergoing destruction and will vote to keep the laws intact for pollution of our air and water.

I had hoped to create a better way to understand how important your voices are when spoken aloud and not hiding in a bedroom behind a computer screen. Come out of your caves folks! We are desperate to meet you and help to guide you to the polling booth without trepidation or fear. I am sure, if you allow the information to soak in, you will be better informed and able to make a difference in all of our lives by just showing up and voting!

I understand that the words "responsibility" and "civic duty" would indeed freak me out as well as it does for many people who do not vote. Perhaps the rebellion and need to thwart the establishment's demands upon us is standing up tall. We face the politicians who are attempting to buy, steal, or quash our votes so as to make elections winnable by the ones who stand to benefit from the elected few. If we could just figure out that the people who are trying to scare us into not voting, or making it harder for us to do so are in control. These are the chumps who would have their money and businesses thrive at the expense of the middle class that has failed to express their opinions by not voting.

5

I could think of almost every election in the past 20 years that had been very different than when I began voting in 1972. I have noticed that the media and airwaves had, all of a sudden, allowed lies twisted facts. I have seen hateful propaganda all over the TV that confuses voters. Messing with your brain is what these ads are designed to do.

I remember in a Mass Media class I took in 1973, the subliminal messages delivered in reading material were not as effective as the pumping of colorful, carefully created television commercials, and political ads. I also remember that during those days, the Orson Wells "War of the Worlds" broadcast FCC ruling to identify the broadcast throughout the shows. Because of the panic that ensued, the FCC used this as an example and was still a high priority in stopping panic throughout populations in the USA. We were far more interested in broadcasting the truth more, and the propaganda less.

But, remember, this country is founded on very dirty deeds. We have been quite insane over the years, and the wars versus peacetime are still ridiculous. Really? 239 years as a country and at war for 217 of those years? Man, we have a hang-up with wars, don't we?

If each one of us looks at the whole picture, we realize that we are not as smart as we have been professing all over the world. The rest of the civilized countries laugh at our insanity, and yet we are the first call when there is trouble. I think, we make more weapons because we are always willing to play with our war toys at any given moment. It seems like the USA policing the globe is so much fun, that we keep escalating our power, and domain, so it appears. And of course, the rest of the world knows that we spend 68% of our budget on war toys, keeping wars going for profit, and just general tough-guy attitudes. Typical of the Americans, so says the rest of the world.

We are well-known for being brash, rude, obnoxious, and forceful. Just like the same dudes in Texas running around Europe slapping folks on the back and being discourteous. We seem to think it is our right to cruise all over the world and push people around, but the change is happening, and we all see that the rest of the world is not as amused as they used to be.

It would mean that our voting prowess has not reached any achievement yet, or we are still pretty dang confused about how to do the voting thing without feeling like a complete idiot. The reason the USA wars keep going on is that we have unknowingly, (and knowingly) allowed criminals elected into office. It is our fault, and we know it.

Complaining about the hassle, the studying of laws and proposals, the time consumed, or rebellion makes no sense. The solution: VOTING. Especially if it pisses someone off that, you will bother to do so.

We are all unable to inform the younger people as to how and why the voting in our country works. I have been trying to explain the process to adults, and they are having a problem with the concept. Each and every voter has no idea of how the laws and processes put in place, and over the years rigged

Chapter 2
Do we get a choice?

Could there be a way to allow the simplistic method of choosing a leader surpass the fears of massive information packets? Will there be a better way to slim down the thousands of words regarding a candidate's qualifications or past voting records? This book is a simple guide to understanding how to differentiate between truths and lies while doing the right thing by voting.

When the regular high school student is taking a civics class, the teacher spends a large amount of time trying to explain the way the government works. Currently, the kids in school are even more perplexed because the criminal acts of suppression, gerrymandering, and purchased votes that are staring us all in the face daily. We see this on television, we see the criminals get away with the crimes, and we see the politicians getting elected even though they are under indictment.

Is it possible for us to be able to by-pass the curtain that has the "Powerful Oz" behind it? Is it possible to stop listening to our parents, bosses, husbands, wives, TV, or family members for a moment to derive our opinions? You bet there is. For some folks, the voting process will be an academy award performance to the abovementioned people who would want to sway

9

your vote. You will be required to lie to their faces, and tell them what they want to hear so as to give yourself the private moment where nobody knows who you voted for in that little booth.

This part of the process has always excited me. I walked into a predominately "red" room as my polling place with little old ladies ages 85+ manning the tables wearing their Republican Red. I strolled in with my Democrat Blue outfit, fully prepared with more ID than God, the angry stares began, and it just pisses them off that they cannot control me. Most times, these folks will state that I am not on the register (usually because my name is Italian, and they have no clue how to spell a foreign name), but I watched the frustration in their eyes as they found my name on the registration, and HAD to let me vote. Wearing every Democratic badge, and sporting my Democrat Blue, I snickered each time I passed through another barrier where they would want to stop me. I know it pisses them off, and I do enjoy their scrunched up faces, and curt tone of voice.

Upon appearing after my vote, my dedication to MAKING SURE my ballot was in the correct box, and nobody could take it away, lose it, or magically deem it un-countable was diligent. I would ask loudly if my ballot tallied correctly, only to watch them scurry to make sure I received a receipt and as I bade them farewell, my excitement spread all over my face with a huge smile and a "check you people later" farewell. I would take a photo in front of the polling area, and a mention of my whereabouts then added to my total back-up of my voting process, so as to not be denied. I always walk away from the polling booth totally thrilled, excited, and counted as a citizen of the USA.

You see, I am one who had to fight for the right to vote for 18-year-olds in 1970-71 because they were sending 18-year-olds to Viet Nam without having any say in the war starting in general. We had to wait until we were 21 at that point, so it was imperative that we had a part in the choosing of the leaders. The act of involvement politically is the reason I am so concerned with the complacency of the younger folks, and even the people my age as Baby Boomers. I am wondering what makes this process so intimidating that we would rather just not participate. Could there be more to the act of not voting? I certainly think that the whole process is so corrupt that most would like to be a nonconformist, and hopefully that would teach the establishment a lesson. The problem with that logic is the establishment would like you not to vote. They do not want your input because it contradicts their agenda and their personal beliefs. Here is where it gets sticky.

The total concept that not voting is making a difference in how the elections turn out is correct. BUT not the way you would like it. This action (or shall I say non-action) is the reason the corruption is flowing without prosecution currently. It seems that the politicians are so corrupt they don't even hide it anymore.

Sometimes we are just too tired, without a vehicle, or having to work odd hours to be able to get to a polling place. I have been watching many who have just started voting by mail so as to not have to take any time and appear at a place on a certain day at a certain time. Most people are so screwed up in the process that they don't even know they can vote every time the same way if they want. We have received many ways to achieve a vote in our country, but the white, conservative male politicians have been very forthright in taking away these methods one by one. The voter's purges alone are a very sad method of eliminating voters, as well as the constant discovery of votes just thrown away or lost if from a predominant Democrat precinct. From the moment the laws get re-worded, the gerrymandering or redistricting comes into play.

The conservative states are aware of who lives where and what affiliation they have with each party. It is to their advantage to make a person drive 45 miles to a polling booth and not bat an eye that the process may be a little too excessive. The Voter's rights Act was a good thing to have aided the people who have no way of getting to a polling booth. They have trouble acquiring proper ID for the cost or incapable of providing a birth certificate because some are 90 years old or never had one. Even though most of these older folks have been voting for 60+ years, they are being denied their constant right because of the paperwork now required is excessive.

So, before you even start to register, the deck is stacked against you. What a rotten thing to have to deal with before you even get a chance to voice your opinion or cast a vote. And I am here to change the whole process into something that can be fun, exhilarating, and accomplishing.

If the act of voting is so repulsive to people and the reason is that nothing ever passes or people elected that we wanted, well that is silly. If the measures, officials, and issues DO pass, then the masses have spoken. How can you derive the total population of voters for the small amount who do vote? If some citizens voting are only 37% of the population who is eligible to vote, then how would the elected officials and laws be the population of citizens speaking out? It would not be the masses speaking, but the folks who are diligent in the act of doing the voting task, and dealing with the results.

We will all feel better when we know that the largest amount of people speaks out by voting, and not the few who consider themselves "privileged" or in control of the populous. The fact is, we do not have to worry about the rest of the people out there doing their civic duty, but we do have to worry about the fact that the voters are not the voice of our country.

Did you hear that? THE VOTERS ARE NOT THE VOICE OF THE USA. The real people out in the land are not participating for numerous reasons. The bad news is, the reasons are sometimes the result of the gerrymandering and redistricting as well as voter ID laws that create more hassle for citizens with more cost. Or the purging ways in which eligibility remains determined, which can create more complications while ruling out past voting prowess over a 60 year period for some older voters.

The Supreme Court's foolish ruling in eliminating the Voter's Rights Act has caused a very difficult climb for those in the same states that needed this law in the first place. Remember, the Act was created to protect the voters from the very same thing that is occurring right now. Yes, we are repeating history, and it is VERY bad news for the citizens of our country.

Chapter 3
Nobody has time

Looks like the younger people have the same comments about voting as, the older folks. Most think that by not voting they are making a statement. Well to me, your statement is that you do not care what happens to all of us out here who find it necessary to speak up. I see that more people will just bitch and moan about the taxes, laws, low wages, no work, or the rich getting richer instead of doing something about it. I don't mean you have to go out and protest, even though it would be nice to see your faces out here fighting for what is not corrupt or criminal in our government system.

Most will sit back and smoke a fatty while commenting about how things used to be and how nice it would be if our life were as simple as it was 60 years ago. Bullshit. We had a VERY hard time back then, and the folks who think this way are usually frightened or beaten down to nothing but excuses.

What was it that made them so sure our way of life was better when we had race riots, KKK, horrible wars, death from back alley abortions, lynch mobs, and murders daily? You see, we have tried to overcome the terrible things our country has done to humans starting with the Indians genocide and moving along to the citizens who happen to be of color. What the heck is wrong with this country? Why is it we cannot seem to move forward while the Civil War crowd keeps chanting "the South will rise again"…?

Keep in mind that they all will finally die of old age, and the movement of younger people will try to mend the large rip in our citizen's flag of democracy. So break out your sewing needles people, we are about to create a new way of dealing with the corruption by voting he Hell out of the place!

Starting with the way we look at voting, we can change the attitude in being incompetent at the pools. We can learn about the ways to make a change in our system by simply learning which candidate is the crook. Currently, it is more than a hassle to do the research, but if we could just eliminate the media crap and do a little reading, we could change our thought process. But if reading is not your thing, maybe it's time that we all start to pay attention to the voting being done by whom and for what purpose. If a person were to take a moment away from gaming, or Facebook, the research is right there at your fingertips. No, not the thousands of memes posted with more than lies and "talking points", but the actual voting by your representatives. You know the people who work for you.

I heard a politician say this week "you never saw a rich person working for a poor person". Well, this is totally untrue. They (the rich politicians) ARE working for us, the poor people in our country. They are our employees. Yes,

OUR representatives who WE elected to represent us. So, why is it that these people in office only represent the rich? It's our fault. We, the people have been duped because we are not paying attention.

Not one of the people in office who is trying to take away all of our rights has been a proper representative to their constituents. Not one. How could people get into office who would take away our Social Security when we have paid our whole lives into it? How can they take away our voting rights and make it harder for us to vote? How can they change laws so we cannot even speak the words "Climate Change"? How can they deem that Christianity is the only religion in the world, and all who are not Christians must die? How can they say women are inferior and must be subservient to males? What the heck is going on here?

The concept that a pile of dudes who are sitting around in a darkened room, drinking their brandy, have decided these things without any of us approving is nauseating. I want to puke. It makes me feel like giving up and running to another country where people are treated fairly, and life is based on human needs and not as much greed and corruption. Our country is embarrassing, and I for one have no more patience with these sick and underhanded people in office.

If you think I am talking about our Democratic President, you are incorrect. You have undergone brainwashing thinking that the Democrats are just as bad as the GOP. Not one Democrat wants to abolish Social Security, take away women's rights, deny climate change, oppress voting, or stop wages from increasing. Not one. If you think that this book is about how to be a liberal, perhaps you need a few more chapters to understand that the only people interested in the Grand Old Party are the wealthy people. And we know why.

Chapter 4
I don't feel like it.

To start the process of wanting to vote, we must understand that we do not have to vote if we don't want to. This way, we think the futile feelings of our vote, not counting will go away. I think that the whole process has become so complicated that younger people feel like they are in another civics class and have to study subjects for hours to be able to vote. This is not true. We can sift through the crap, and find the reasoning for any issue, or candidate without having to spend hours or days trying to decipher what the information pamphlets are saying.

When they send you the big book and your sample ballot most of you will cringe and set it on the table to "get back to it later". Here is the problem. The ominous size and the obvious amount of time that you will have to spend digesting this book should come with college credits. Most of us will look through a couple of pages and sigh in boredom. Another amount of folks will have already made their choice long before the book arrives because of a large amount of media blitzing with campaign ads. But these ads are ALL deceiving. We had better pay more attention.

We haven't got too much time in our lives to spend reading junk that arrives through the mail or e-mail, so we start deleting what we should be reading. I do think that the continuous amount of crap pumped through the airwaves and the junk sent to us is for one purpose. The media blitzes are designed to sway you to think the way someone else does. Well, that does not work for me, and I am hoping it won't work for any of you either.

I am sure we can all find a way to express ourselves through voting. Perhaps finding an easier and more exciting way to speak your mind through the ballot is in order so as to create a feeling of accomplishment when leaving the polling booth. I know I do a happy dance each time I vote because I know I have my presence counted and even if I am not the winner in a certain issue, I know I made my statement clear to the USA. So maybe that is just a cheap thrill I get when voting.

I mean, how is it that I can walk out of the booth and shout "whoo-hoo" when I know that someone has to listen to me, and no matter who is trying to deceive me, I have seen through their evil plans. I have taken the time to make sure the facts are not "Fox talking points" and my conclusions continue to remain educated, fact checked, and relevant to every issue.   I have also been thrilled when I discover the vast majority of people are thinking the same as I do. Currently, we must always remember that the people in our country are far more apt to vote for something that concerns them. Being wealthy is only a small 1% margin, and the current purchasing of elections show all of us how important it is to vote.

They (the conservative GOP and Tea Party folks) will also attempt to quash everyone who does not vote for their self-centered laws. Remember, if you are a person who does not fall into the 1%, the remaining population is vast. If we all would just take a moment and send in a ballot instead of boycotting voting, we could be moving at a tremendous pace forward. The right wing conservatives are rich, the rest of us are just getting by without the end in sight. That would take each and every one of us out of the GOP and vote our conscience, and not by our pocketbook contents.

The process can be a fun thing when you know that you have thwarted the people who would want citizens without Social Security, no HealthCare, no living wages, and no access to women's care, no access to voting, no civil rights, and no human rights. Yes, I for one have left the polling booths many times knowing I have pissed off a bunch of conservative blowhards who would want me oppressed, pregnant, and barefoot in a kitchen my whole life. I am a rebellious individual, and through voting I have been able to state my position many times.

Sometimes the people vote against their interests and end up in dire straits. The comments from the poor who vote for GOP are so mixed up and confused. The women who vote GOP are usually so oppressed that they have no real concept of what or why they are voting. Most wives or girlfriends continue to vote the way their husbands or boyfriends want them to vote. Most have no idea how issues affect them. "Oh sure, I'll vote for whoever you say honey pie." More people, especially younger people and women need to spend more time and learn how each politician and issue enters our lives.

At some point, we haven't been informed properly nor have we evaluated the contents of the propositions or issues we vote on. Some issues are not relevant to each, but if we just look at how the impact affects others, we can be better voters. Sometimes a vote for an educational issue seems irrelevant to a person like me who has no children. Although I pay taxes for educational systems, I have never sent a child to school. But, I am concerned with the kids who come out of school as adults that cannot even spell or think critically, so I am happy to pay for education. Most who have left high school and were in the workforce have not a clue about balancing a checkbook, paying bills, voting, writing a resume, critical thinking, political science, applying for jobs, or anything relevant to their lives. We teach them nothing to get them ready for a working world.

Sure, we teach them to add and subtract, read and write, but what should we be teaching kids? Why does it always seem that the things we need to teach are being kicked out a curriculum because the conservatives do not want the kids to know about sex, birth control, true history, racism in our country, or how to survive without a job? Why would a person deny a child the information to make a successful life? Hmmm. Think about it for a moment. "If I can make sure the children who are coming out of school have no knowledge, then I can control and enslave them." Says the wealthy lawmakers and their cohorts. If we keep them stupid, we can use them until they become ill and die. Keep the Healthcare away from them, and they will die sooner. Keep the birth control away from them so they will multiply and provide the "boss man" more slaves. And, folks, this is happening in 2015! WE ARE SMARTER THAN THIS. I presume we are all just lazy, and would like to have nothing to do with the energy that does not flow right into our hands. I got mine, get your own. Sadly, we are selfish people, and this is not a healthy way to interact with other humans.

I would like to extend the high school curriculum to include items that would help a child enter the adult world with a little better perspective and some useful skills. I know that I did not have any of these wonderful learning tools and had to learn this on my own. Most of us do. I would like to think that if we received better tools and learned more about adult skills, each one of us would be thrilled to vote to have our voices heard.

I would also tend to believe that our destiny is not to die with the most money, but to have made a mark and helped others to survive.

We have slowed in assistance to our fellow man, and the results are beginning to become more obvious to more people as time passes. We have changed our views on things over the years due to evolving while the earth and its contents change. Why can't we see that the "rich and powerful" people are still just people? They have nothing different than we and cannot possibly be made more valuable to an organism that is exactly the same. Money is invisible folks, and those that are obsessed with it are insane. Money equals debt. Nothing more, nothing less. Now get a clue, and think about this for a moment. It may make you angry enough to DO something about the value system on this planet. I say, think about the resources first. Save and preserve, as well as replace the resources you take away. That way, people in the future will be able to enjoy the wonderful pleasures of food and water.

Chapter 5
Voter's Information more like Voter Overload.

The ability to understand the [junk] that is in a voter's information pamphlet can be very time-consuming. There are so many confusing comparisons in the voter's pamphlet and the act of figuring out what they mean remains impossible. Most of the information is written sideways like they do in Motor Vehicle testing. The yes vote means no, and the no vote means yes, for example. I remember how the gay marriage Proposition 8, carefully written sideways when they had a re-vote in California in 2008. Most of us thought we were voting yes on gay marriage, and that was not the case. The issue was written so as to have a yes vote mean "yes we do not want gay marriage". Now that is just sneaky. Luckily the SCOTUS changed the whole thing, and California is finally a place where you can marry who you want. But for a long time, we were all furious because the 1st series (in 2008) proposition was written with the intent to confuse the voter.

I have become very angry each time I find that the voting words are juggled to mean something other than what a common person can understand. I now get the idea that the people who want to control me are writing the issues and propositions to where nobody can understand them. Oh, the memories of the Jim Crowe testing era for voting. The tests were designed to make sure nobody could answer correctly and thus eliminating a lot of voters. I do understand that this process currently in use, executed by writing laws, propositions, and issues sideways so that none of us can vote rationally and logically. The remainder of the word juggling has made the act of voting seem insignificant. At this point, the voter becomes frustrated and just chooses not to participate based upon total confusion or excessive complication.

Each time we head to the voting booth, there should be an air of excitement and accomplishment. Like finishing a class and getting an "A". The world is at your feet if you speak out, and the wonderful feeling of helping others by getting the corrupt rich out of office with term limits should make your heart soar.

But then there are people who believe that the rich will provide them with jobs, or will share their wealth somehow. So, with this reasoning, the USA should go back to the days of the Civil War before women could vote, or even the days of non-unions where children of 10 years old were working in factories for 12 hours a day. Sure, there are people who still think that the old days were golden, but at the US Capitol occupants with old age and the 30+ years of career politics, dementia has already set in.

We are not that generation. We do not want to go backwards, and none of us are willing to give up the wonderful things we have fought for over the years. All of us are feeling like we are undergoing testing during this current era of wars, corruption, greed, corporate personhood, and civil rights violations. Each one of us is valuable in that we are into a situation where if we don't vote the career politicians out, our future is dead, and so are we.

See? Making that one little effort to vote and make the evil crap go elsewhere (like back to the Neanderthal cave dwellings) is what the purpose of the vote is all about. We can make the horrible laws stop, the influence of wealthy people making our decisions for us stop, and the people who perpetuate the conservative archaic ways stop. We can do this, folks. I know we can.

Each one of us is valuable to the society by our interest in making our world a better place and not watch it go to the rich slave owners again. We face this attitude again, even years after slavery abolished in 1865. The rich want us to serve them; they want to keep the wages low, and dependency on assistance intact. Now, don't you think this is totally stupid? Man, I cannot even think of one person I have ever met who was rich enough to play games with the Grand Old Party. I have met thousands of people, and only a few of them had enough money to join that exclusive Conservative, Rich Boy Club. The poor redneck will keep voting the same fools into office hoping that maybe the conservatives will send them a check, get them a job, help them, feed them, or something for their vote.

So, thinking that other people will have your back in voting is completely incorrect. I have a couple of friends who do not vote. They are always very glad when the things or people I have voted for are in office, but they did not participate. Is this the way that some of you are thinking? Do you think that if you let others make the decisions for you by voting, they will have your identical view? Oops. Not the case. You can never rely on the sinister people to think about you or your individual situation. Some will vote the way you would, but that is not enough. You need to participate and show them that they are not in control and that we, the people, are here to prove our power by voting.

Could it be that the process is just too time consuming, or you are not aware of the real issues that are up for a vote? I am sure that if you can order a pizza over the phone, go out for a drink, or run to the store for a snack the process of dropping in and voting shouldn't be a problem. But it is a problem, and I know why.

.

Chapter 6
Too solemn and negative

I know why you don't or won't vote. It is not because any of you are incapable, but the process is very unnerving and confusing. None of us want to make a mistake or screw things up with such a seemingly solemn process like voting. I mean, that stuff is "worldly" and very responsible. Bullshit. Think about how a bunch of words on a page could scare you. It can't unless the words read "You are under arrest, or Taxman is looking for you." They are a bunch of words. The fear of what the responsibility of a vote for or against is what scares people. Thinking that perhaps a wrong vote could mean devastation for your family or yourself. The panic of not understanding what the words mean to you and your family is what seems frightening. "How can I not know what this means?" I would say to myself. How am I confused about the no vote meaning yes and the yes vote meaning no? See? There is a method to how the people who write the propositions, issues, and information pamphlets. I would tend to believe that the confusion in how to vote has been a DMV tactics for years. I would also profess that the voting information is as vague as you can imagine, and the intent is to confuse the reader. I smell Jim Crowe laws…

The lawmakers have made the laws so complicated that none of us look forward to reading that insane voter's pamphlet. The dang thing is about 4 inches thick and looks like something that I have used in my Political Science classes for a textbook. I can remember looking through my first voter's pamphlet and trying to understand who was running with which platform, but the words were so confusing I couldn't understand what it meant. I spent a large amount of time trying to read the whole thing and realized a brief summary eliminating the excess verbiage would have been better absorbed. They could have been broken down to a few specific sentences.

If you look at the candidates sections, you will find that the individual and their merits are well written with no confusion. But, if you start to look at the issues, propositions, or measures, things start to get confusing. The result in elections going odd directions is what the conservatives or right wing folks want to have happened to a voter. They want you so confused that you will pretty much screw up the vote by not voting on the issue, or voting incorrectly of your intent. The act of confusing the voter remains a constant, and it looks to me that the writing of these ballot measures and lawmaking procedures have a specific agenda in words. The need to be able to decipher what the law says, and what the law or proposition means is the secret to voting clean and efficiently.

Each one of us can read a sentence and figure out the meaning, but when information is compiled so as to deceive or confuse a person, the trouble sets in. I remember voting in California in 2011 with Proposition 19 to legalize weed and have the farmers pay income taxes, but the way it was written made it hard to calculate the yes vote versus the no vote. We lost that vote because people didn't understand the way the issue read. Of course since then, the state is comfortable with weed and even though it was brought to a vote, we were screwed in 2011.

Currently, the Ohio Marijuana Initiative the voters voted against the legalization of marijuana because the law was written screwy. The local state billionaires wanted to have a monopoly on the growing. Luckily, the voters struck down the measure, not because of anti-legalization, but because the law remains written so as to benefit the greedy corporations instead of the people.

The changing of wording, adding and subtracting items of concern is what I am saying here. Being able to figure out which law is written sideways and which law makes sense to our existence is the basis for learning how to vote.

We can take the issues and break them down into categories. Simply, we would take the state issues, local issues, and representatives of our constituency and write them down. Under each measure find the one or two things it means for you and your family in the city you live. Next, take the state measures and do the same. Look for the basic and simple summary of the state's request for more money and apply it to your personal needs. Not the needs of the corporations, or big businesses (unless you are one of them), but the needs of you and your family. The corporations will remain wealthy, so you don't have to worry about the business failing. Nor do you all have to worry about corporations unable to hire people if you make them pay higher taxes, as this statement is untrue. If you are paying attention, the wealthy does not pay anywhere near as much taxes as you do percentage wise.

So, perhaps your concern for the wealthy by voting their "puppets" into office is where your life becomes screwed. If you are not aware of how their wealth affects you and your family, perhaps a quick jaunt through Google will enlighten you. You can look up facts that are not propaganda from the right wing, and look for the facts on issues and not the opinions from the "radio and TV clowns" Let me give you an example of unbiased and factual articles online or websites not based upon religion, hate, or uncivil behavior. Reuters, Al Jazzier, Wiki news, Alter Net, The Real News, The Independent, PBS, BBC, and C-SPAN gives all the information without the "spins". Nobody is telling you that you will go to Hell if you don't believe them, nor will there be anything that will make you feel ignorant. Maybe it is better to be informed without the baggage.

Most of us can figure out when someone is bullshitting them, and most of us are rolling our eyes each time someone comes up with a way to hurt, degrade, humiliate, steal from, or murder another person legally. I think that our common sense is pretty intact, and we all do have some logic instilled in us from somewhere in our early lives. But remember, there are people who are sucked into that vacuum that has no air.

The people who have been radicalized and subdued to believe most anything a rich person, or person with power (usually they go hand in hand) says as truth, are lost. Why would these people lie to me? Why would someone tell me that I was no longer going to have health insurance, or that my women's clinics were being taken away even though I need them for regular health issues and not abortions? Why would someone tell me that I was not able to make as much money as a dude if I was doing the same job? Why are they trying to take away my Social Security when I paid my whole life into the system? Why don't they want me to have healthcare? Why would someone think that I would be happy giving up all my rights so as to have nothing left but death in my future?

I cannot understand how it is possible for people to run off a cliff like Lemmings and follow someone around who could care less about them. The thought that people blindly become enamored by a politician who is removing every right earned over hundreds of years while doing it with a smile on their face sickens me. "Oh don't worry, this won't happen to you... just the 'other' people if you vote for me". So it goes without saying.

There is no reason for anyone to vote just because someone has told them it will better their lives. You don't have to vote because you think it's the right thing to do. You should vote to CHANGE things for everyone, not just yourself. The vote you will donate to bad people will only help them, and not you or your family. Please try to remember the only thing that should concern you is how your vote will help you and your family. Not which politician or wealthy billionaire will know you voted for them and were grateful? They do not care about you after the vote, only before. Remember that you are very important to them before an election, but if you are of color, female, young, or the slightest bit liberal you have just eliminated your chance of having your voice heard. They will do anything to make sure you do not vote and have many ways to do this.

The re-writers of the laws will then create new methods by redistricting, gerrymandering, oppression, voter ID laws, voter purging, lost ballots, electronic voting failures, and crap that makes it impossible while counted as a valid ballot. It is your job as a citizen, even if you do not vote, to call out these people and make voting easier for all of us. Making it difficult has been the mantra of the GOP since the Voter's Rights Acts in 1965 was signed. And of course, thank you to the SCOTUS for eliminating our one protection for the shenanigans going on currently. Boy, are they getting this ready for the theft of the 2016 election. They did it with G.W. Bush both times, and I am certain that they are getting their corruption, thievery, suppression, lost votes, purged votes, and deception all warmed up so as to destroy all we have worked for as soon as possible. We seem to bust them, and nothing remains accomplished. We all can see that the rigged system while meddled with, and nobody gets jail time or undergoes prosecution. How come each of the money people processed or sentenced to prison seem to get out early, have she-she accommodations while behind bars, or do not have to do any time at all for their crimes?

These people must stop so as to save us all from eventual madness. People who are not able to understand what being a regular person in the USA is really like are trying to do this to us. The Koch brothers, as well as many other perpetrators of monetary corruption, have had their wealth handed to them by inheritance. None of them have a clue how the real world lives, and just like the movie "Trading Places", I would love to give Mortimer and Randolph a dose of poverty and have their fortunes wiped out just to piss them off for a change. I am tired of being part of those who are always suffering from what the wealthy has laid upon us.

We need to understand that we have the power. The wealthy are relying on money as a value system, and we are falling for it. We believe that we are worthless because we are not the 1%, we believe that we have nothing to offer unless we make money or are paid. The offering of money in exchange for ideas, skills, trades, natural talents, and innovations have seen a reduced to a "minimum wage" and no cost of living increases. You see, the wealthy have planned this, and we have just gone right along with it like we were sheep. So very sad to see the people of our country and the world, then reduced to a mere pile of dollars and cents. Ah, the Monetary System. A ridiculous deceit next to the religious fraud. And of course, we are all falling for the same crap, different year.

There will be outstanding potential leaders who will not be able to come up with the billions it seems to take to be elected nowadays, which still perplexes me. I have understood that we will never see a good person who is not stinking rich be able to lead, even though they would be perfectly qualified or just one of us. I only wish that a regular person could run for office. You know, someone who had to struggle and get through life, understanding how the majority of the country lives. We cannot allow this to happen again in our life unless we change the voting process and also eliminate the dirty money going to these pre-ordained political clowns. All of them.

It appears that the only way we can get back our lives is to fight and make the rules applicable to all people, not the corporate personhood people or the wealthy contributors to the super PACs by VOTING. Get the Dirty Money out of the system, and we can go back to where we left off. Busting every banker, and throwing the book on the people who would choose to enslave other humans. We stopped that years ago, how can we possibly be up to the same nonsense again? I'll bet it has something to do with ignorance and false senses of security.

So it also seems that the people who are manipulating the money rules are also the same people who make it more difficult for citizens to vote. I am certain that the majority of the people out in the voting world are not the least bit sure if their vote will even be tallied. Most of us are always a little skeptical about the people we see taking our very precious ballot away to a box. I suppose you can get a receipt for voting now, and apparently with some of the shenanigans amidst the obvious states, there is a problem.

As I have walked into polling places and looked at the workers, I always think to myself that these people are just as prone to make the numbers "go away" or have the ballots disappear. We could never be certain that the precinct would be one that become disqualified for certain regional restrictions. None of us would even be able to tell if the voting we participated in is the actual counted and correct votes tally.

What makes any of you people out there in readership land think that the voting scene isn't rigged to the max? Or that the rigging is now being flaunted all over the place, right in our view, bragging on social media, and taunting the authorities just to try to catch them. I offer the point that brings the question to light. The question that every person has in their mind as they think about voting and the process. "Does my vote count?" (Really????) Does it count to where I can believe I am not being fooled to believe that the voting is just an appeasement so that I won't protest or have a fit? People, think about it. The reason they have to appease the masses is because an uprising can take place with success when executed by millions of people. The money people have successfully made a little nest in our minds and has begun to hatch a few bad eggs. It is up to all of us to believe that the vote is making, at least, a statement and perhaps a voice that would be heard by others.

Oh for goodness sakes. We are just falling into the trap set by the same people who have perpetuated the money lies. All of us have to take some responsibility for the same greed we have in that we want more, more, more. We want what others have. We want to have the current gadget or electronic device. We strive to get more, have more, and want more. I do believe that this is a very bad and tedious process to be caught up. I also think that we have the power to change the way we think about money. Is it possible that we can take what we have in resources and replace, replenish, and enhance the same? Can we be intelligent enough to see that petroleum products are finite? They WILL run out. Then what? I keep asking the same question to those who would not want to find other methods of energy.

We have a dedication to the survival of life on this planet, and we have ruthlessly destroyed and eliminated species. We have spilled unnatural toxins and petroleum into the water supplies. The masses have ignored the fracking chemicals thrust into the earth's crust. The results of this act have become the basis in which we all must act quickly by voting the laws in to protect the environment. We NEED to do this so as to help replenish the earth in what we have taken.

Chapter 7
Bitching does help a little

Now, I know this looks like a liberal's bashing of conservatives, but somehow the voting process has been destroyed by none other than the conservatives. Nobody else is trying to do this act of anti-democratic activity. I want a dang "Bitchfest", and I am going to do so throughout this whole book, so maybe it does help to let things out. Why would these people be so concerned with voter's rights? Why would someone want to take away the thing that our country was initially based upon as a democracy? How come I am always looking at the Grand Old Party for doing such evil and dysfunctional things to disallow citizens to have a voice and shout their discontent? Of course, the answer is MONEY.

The purchasing power of that stupid little piece of worthless paper. The thing that makes people kills one another. The one thing that will change the logical and sensible person's mind to jelly seems to be the vision of wealth brought forth by the conservative party. Do we think that we will be rich when we grow up? Do we not realize that the wealth of today is pretty much just inherited and not earned? And the people who work their way to wealth by struggling, paying their dues, and succeeding are not conservatives by nature. Most of the entrepreneurs are very liberal and would do anything to help the people. I have read many excerpts from "new rich" people who dedicate themselves to helping others and sharing their wealth. How come NONE of the conservatives are generous? Why are so-called "conservative" people insisting on keeping the wealth away from the regular people? I think we are all very sure that the hoarding, greed, gluttony, selfishness, and elitist attitudes play a large part. The need to make sure the rich are up on their pedestal with the rest of us in servitude is obviously their desire, and somehow we have been very nice to allow them to tread all over us. I think that this must stop. And voting will do the trick. Big time.

So it seems that the people who would have each one of us give up what we have earned or fought for over the past two centuries. The control, wealth, and power are the directives that most politicians are learning. I think that we can differentiate between the scoundrels and the good people. I don't think we are all that stupid to believe everything we hear on the radio or TV. Wouldn't you all think that if someone tells you that voting for the richest guy would get you a paycheck, we all would just laugh? I know people on Social Services still waiting for their Republican Party checks to arrive, just because they voted for the clowns.

We are all aware of the process of dumbing down America, but the people are starting to become more informed about the Internet researching as well as the different ways we are now fact checking bullshit. There cannot be another way to flush out the liars, cheaters, greedy, corrupt, or wannabe's but to do it in large groups, and hold fast on to the truth. Do not let the Nay Sayers provoke you into believing that the more you pay the rich people, the more you will get at the end. I think they meant their idea of the end, and not yours. Also, which one of you believes that "trickle-down economics" worked? You need to get a clue and notice, it is not working, nor has it ever worked. Reagan was a total fool and more than likely already had Alzheimer's way before his diagnosis, but at least did his entire scam job with a smile and a joke. ("I do not recall, I do not recall, I do not recall" at the Iran-Contra hearings).

Perhaps our views have been skewed so that we don't trust anyone who is in office. I think we have been screwed so many times by those in office that we are all sick and tired of dealing with the voting altogether. We could have realized a long time ago that the reason things are so crappy in the government situation is because we didn't bother to vote the helpful measures or people into office. I continuously blame the non-voters for a large amount of problems in our political arenas, but that is not enough. We have been voting as much as we can and have also been unsuccessful to elect more competent people to represent us.

The problem could be that the people running have purchased all the votes they need to remain in their positions for years and years, as well as being bought and sold via lobbyists. I remember when the lobbyists were not allowed to bribe politicians, but that went away somehow with some dark back room voting by the Congress.

Another entity that has changed dramatically in the election process is the tons of terribly offensive ads running on TV. How many times can you bad mouth someone and make me believe that the information spewed is close to being the truth? How many times do I have to hear a total lie and note that nobody calls the advertisers on the total absurdity of the commercial? How do we look at a certain candidate and understand that the advertisement running is meant to do the opposite, in fact, presentation?

I am not amused, and not so easily fooled by the commercials. I mean, look at the BP commercial telling us all that the "Gulf is back to normal". Total lie. Complete fabrication and the Gulf is in terrible shape thanks to BP and their mess. This advertisement is running over and over even though WE ALL KNOW it's crap.

The people who would want us all ill, destitute, impoverished, enslaved in labor, and dying remains the whole diversionary tactic of the political scene. They will do anything and say anything to make you think, they care and things are rosy. And I know they also believe that if they repeat the lie over and over, it will suddenly become the truth. So, now the fun begins. I will be happy to be a rebel, and make more trouble for the wealthy, white, males who seem to think that we are all stupid and uninterested.

Oh boy, are they in for trouble.

Chapter 8.
Do I want the power?

WE HAVE THE POWER. We can change this rich versus poor thing. We can change the black versus white, male versus woman straight versus gay, and multiple other foolish hate wars against each other. If some of us can get off our butts for a moment and execute an opinion or a vote, we can be prosperous too.

I am talking about taking back what the wealthy has removed from "We, the People". They have totally destroyed the environment so we cannot breathe or drink water. They have polluted the air and killed off the animal life with the extinction of many species of animals. They have created an oligarchy that removes all of our rights based on our being poor.

But they have not removed our right to vote yet. They HAVE attempted to make it so hard and complicated that complacency has ensued. But we can start to WAKE UP and figure out this is all a very serious plan to put the USA back to the Civil War days, where white supremacy, oppression of women and slavery was the law of the land.

I believe that none of us are ready for slavery, nor are we ready to have large camps to harbor our citizens in servitude. Indentured servants are illegal, and still we are slaves of the money and greed that propels the continuous circle of greed and corruption in our country.

The fun part of involving oneself in civil unrest is the way that the conservatives twitch and squirm with uneasy feelings. We want people to have a problem with the ways that harm others, and treat humans as slaves. We have a problem with the way the rich or very foolish people have taken over every facet of voting by creating impossible hurdles to jump over to be even allowed near the process. We know that the rich and affluent people want desperately to be the only people voting (like in the early years of our history) only to find that this cannot be taken back 239 years. We cannot allow the women's vote removed, nor the black vote, or the youth vote, or any vote. We earned these rights by suffering, protesting, being killed, and still they want to remove them from our grasps. How can we fix this?

We can continue to use the means and methods in which we fought. We can remember the many who had fought and died for these rights. We cannot forget how these many things came to pass. We will not re-write history, but we will find out which parts of history have been suppressed and told incorrectly. We will correct the many lies that we have been living for hundreds of years, by acknowledging that they exist and need to be made truthful and clear to all.

The secret is not to let the ones who would oppress your vote know that you are aware of their tactics. I do so enjoy knowing more about law and the applicable uses of my voting skills far better than the people sitting in the polling places judging me each time I walk in. I enjoy knowing more facts than fiction, and will vote accordingly. I am totally thrilled understanding that my vote for local and statewide issues were thought out and considerate of the rest of the population I reside within my voting area.

I am a very educated voter, and will not fall for totally illogical actions, and rights earned stripped away from my fellow citizens. I am there to protect those who cannot vote or will not vote. It is also my duty to teach voting to those who are afraid or not interested in their involvement civic duty minded elections. If we all took a moment throughout our raising our children or grandchildren to explain to them how exciting being a voting citizen will be when they grow up, they would all be as thrilled as I am every time they enter a polling place.

But the parents failed us, and the generations proceeded to diminish in their active voting actions. So, what happened? Did things get so hard or complicated that nobody wanted to participate? Or maybe the rebellion in stating that some people will not vote because nobody represents them or their views are present? Or what if they were not voting because "it doesn't do any good anyway"? Maybe they want you to think that they don't register because they don't want to do jury duty? I can think of a hundred very foolish and unbelievable reasons for not voting, but I continue to vote in every election. Sometimes I would think that maybe my choice was incorrect or find out later that who I voted for was a scoundrel. Remember, this is nothing but circumstance, and you cannot change people or their greedy nature. You can only hope they have a conscience. The only way to know about your candidate is to check them out and see what issues concern you and your family. Is the information on your candidate choices something that affects you? Is this just another bunch of super PAC money tossed into someone else's crusty old-timers ideas?

If we could answer all the questions, we would be well informed as voters. But the hard part is trying to understand just what the candidates are professing. Could the speeches be full of general statements which mean nothing to me as an individual? Is it true that the past voting history of the candidate was completely ridiculous and wasted millions of tax payer's dollars? Or is this the person who says you cannot say the words "Climate Change" in your state? Maybe the candidate is one who has bankrupted the state and wanted to run your country, but you realize he hasn't got a clue how to run a state yet alone a country. Or perhaps this candidate is the one who has decided to regulate female's bodies while giving rapists parental rights. I say, pay attention to how they have been running their states, or voting in the House as previous elected officials to know what capabilities they possess.

To be able to figure out your state's issues and how they will affect you and your family, you must do a little research. You don't have to study like you are trying to pass a test, but just do a little checking around and find out who the candidates are. Don't play the game of trying to watch TV and let the media decide for you. The media is owned by the wealthy, so the only message given to you is that of wealthy people becoming wealthier. DO NOT watch TV for your political information!

The media will just run paid ads and each of them full of more and more hatred statements, with lies and partial truths broadcast everywhere. Each ad, no matter the affiliation, has more adverse commentary on the opposing candidates that you cannot even tell who is paying for the ad. Then you see the usual little words... PAC. Oh, that explains all of it. The dirty money is paying for all the super PACs commercials, and we have no way of knowing who is doing the ad bashing. The media exposure is getting to be so foolish that our jokes and ridicule are used for a fun time mocking stupid ads on TV. This mass communication blitzing is only having a reverse effect on the people and their votes. We find it all very funny, and none of us are the least bit in fear or cowering in a corner from the propaganda delivered on television. Especially at election time.

Most of us are sick of political ads that are graphic, full of hate, and completely out of touch with the current facts. Most are about the "old days" when Joe Schmo was at a strip club when he was 21, and now that he's 58 he must suffer the consequences by making sure you won't vote for him. Sheesh. I'll bet the majority of the people in office were found drunk in a ditch when they were

18 a few times, but nobody is coughing up that dirt during their elections.

And of course, the concept that a pre-requisite for the conservatives is that a candidate has committed a crime seems insane! What has happened here? How can we be in praise of people who have spent their whole lives trying to figure out how to deceive the American people? The nervousness in trying to change these lies and find the truth becomes more difficult each day. We are all so confused by the way the people are voting against their interests. We are confused by how the possibility of people in office who are obviously corrupt, and we just look at them and say "oh my".

Is this not a call to the people in our country to pay attention and vote them out of office? Do we not need Term Limits to make sure that the same people are not in power who have trampled on our country like it was a pile of grapes? I think that we have the power, and the only way to eliminate the same people in office who have camped out there for the last 30 years is to get them out! We have the power to do this. Somehow we are totally complacent in our duty to not only ourselves but to the rest of the humans in our country. We have successfully re-created a wealth gap from the beginning of the slave era and progressed it forward to the millennium. How did this happen? How is it that the same people who would have owned slaves and cornered the markets in wealth would be back to haunt the law making process with such archaic and old-fashioned methods?

All of the problems as mentioned above continuously nestle in the fact that the people's voices have been suppressed by the same laws that are used to protect them. How many more times must we see the devastation of a group of people in their daily lives? How many children in poverty in our country must we look at to understand that the only protection they have remains "we the people"? I could perhaps better understand the evil and corrupt people if they were to admit the purpose of their role is to kill people and have them enslaved until their death. At least having them admit this is their goal could make the solution easier.

In psychology classes, I was able to understand that the many facets of fallacy fall in the category of critical thinking. To be able to create and live in a fantasy world would take an enormous amount of planning, as well as assistance from others who believe the same. This method is how the political plans work. The people who wish to be in power, call the folks with the money and sell their ideas. Banking on the fact that the wealthy want nothing but to become wealthier, so the contribution is vast. The people who wish to participate in the profits from their personal interests will always be the donors and as well can be the politicians. We realize that the difference is only in the names, wealth standing, and how much the whole corporation tied to the person is profitable. Not one mention about how the laws or juggling of finances is affecting the people, only in how the "bottom line" is making more money for the politician. It does seem that all politicians are interested in how they can fatten up their bank accounts while in office, and create another outlet for their retirement when finished doing damage to our country while in office. The conservatives seem to think this is the best way to be a political person and govern with only one's self-interest in mind. The problem is, we the people have had just about enough. But how much are we going to take?

Chapter 9
"I am mad as Hell, and I'm not going to take it anymore" – (Network)

Well, it is my opinion that getting infuriated enough to do something about your frustrations in living day to day is the best motivator when thinking about voting. Make each and every point that angers you a basis for finding the way to eliminate or change the effect on your life. If you get angry enough, you can indeed lift a car, or throw a rock 100 feet so perhaps the use of this energy is better spent making a difference. You can make this change by channeling your anger into a new way of expressing it. This process can be a good way to make your life better equipped for future elections.

Each time I find something in an article, newspaper, or hear frustrating lies on the TV shows, I take a look at the source. I remember why the press and media make as many statements as possible to anger or frustrate all facets of political leanings. They will say anything to have their press product promoted and will gladly fill the airwaves with paid ads so they can have more revenue. Advertising is the basis for all political propaganda and all channels, newspapers, and radio stations are very quick to take anything they can to keep the money flowing.

Doesn't it seem like each lie that we hear is contradicted by a rebuttal that seems just as far-fetched? Haven't most of us cocked our heads to the side and said, "What did they just say?" I am certain that all of us are totally sick and tired of the commercials and ads that keep coming out that are flatly evil and harassing. Each one is worse than the next. Each candidate is getting angrier and hateful towards their competitors drones on and on. I think that we can take each foolish statement and decipher for ourselves what is crap and what makes sense. But, the politicians have continued to barrage us with tons of commercials cluttering up any chance at a movie or a sports event night after night.

Doesn't it seem stupid to try to figure out who is telling the truth and who isn't? Most of the current candidates trying to run for President have been parading around with the most foolish and antiquated bull I have ever heard. And I have been voting for 43 years. I do not think even the same words were being spoken in the early 70's when I started voting. There were abortion issues, but we solved them. We were tired of seeing women die from botched abortions. There were civil rights issues, but we started addressing and changing these as well. But now, all I am hearing is that women need to go back to being subservient, need no special women's healthcare and need no assistance to feed their children. If they are single mothers, they will need to find a husband, they won't make a living wage if they do work, or the female will always worry about physical assaults if attending college or in public areas now. Black people are under attack by the police, no matter what the situation, police will continue to proclaim war on citizens, no more Social Security, retirement at 70, no Medicare, no Medicaid, and the rest of the crap spewing from their mouths.

These people are hateful, religiously overdone, and have no idea what the rest of the world has already accomplished. We, as a country, have been nothing but backwards and ignorant. We need to pay more attention and try to get things better adjusted to each of our states. We do not need to go backwards in time and watch our rights be taken away one by one. The religious nuts are completely out of line by becoming a "listened to" political basis, yet they do not pay taxes. The billionaires from the Churches are the reason the flood of cash has migrated back and forth from banks to churches to politicians. I, for one, have had enough.

Oh, we must learn to vote for the thrill so as to totally piss off those who would be very quick to put all of us into slavery. I can imagine that all of the negative banishments would be what the rich want, and what the powerful need. They need servants so as to make them feel super rich and wonderfully powerful. Well, I am not one who will go into that servitude easily. I will fight for those who cannot, and for those who refuse.

I always enjoy a good rally, and with this book, I am hoping that each and every one of us will rise and take hold of our rights. We must determine who and what will drive the country forward. We do not want to go backwards, and we also do not want to suffer the way our forefathers did. I am hoping that together, we can all figure out a quick and efficient way to do the ominous chore of voting while knowing when leaving the polling place we will be happy, and contented to have spoken loudly and pissed off many people who deserve to be taken down a notch.

I am not saying that voting is such a rebellion that a person should be radical, but I am saying voting is worth holding on to with a true fight. Heck, maybe being a little radical will wake a few folks up to understand that we are not all here to be lazy and watch the world float past. We cannot have the future dream to be that of a hammock and a beer for the rest of our lives. Don't we have to wake up and do something each morning so as to verify our existence? There are many things that can be accomplished to allow the vast population a way to coexist. We need to tolerate each other without removing individual's rights because of wealth, status, or race.

Voting has got to be something thrilling and exciting. Maybe there is something that makes a citizen a better participant in a functioning democracy. Yes, the usual cliché is voting should be your duty. I hate to say the word because most equate the term "duty" with jury duty, laundry duty, work duty, etc. The way I look at the duty is the same as when I cough and cover my mouth. I don't want to hurt or harm anyone, but I need to cough to satisfy a physical reaction. I need to cover my mouth to be able to protect others from harm. The natural order of democracy is to participate, so the remainder of the people we coexist with will continue to be protected from the condition or disorder of others. It is our duty to rescue a creature from a horrible demise, and it is also our duty to help those who feel oppressed or are unable to speak for themselves.

Maybe another way to look at voting is how much less you will have to protest about when you receive your paycheck or go out and buy groceries. The attempt to just stand back and let others do the voting work indicates just how lazy we are. The necessity of living our lives without hassle is pretty important to all of us nowadays. But, I think we are all guilty of creating more hassle than is truly necessary. Remember that a prediction of gloom is a total waste of time spent enjoying the now.

Perhaps the way we express ourselves in the cities and towns we live in is in question. We have all been exposed to the Internet while surrounded by loads of new information sources. We have been able to find out about other countries, problems in their governments, monetary systems, environmental disasters, and pollutions. For example, then there is an earthquake which creates Tsunami's and devastation, the USA is always right there to help. Then comes the fraud, corruption, and thievery like locusts to prey upon the money sources. The disasters become a fraudulent way to obtain quick cash, and the cycle begins again for every disaster on the planet.

We haven't quite grasped the routine well enough to stay out of the line of fraud fire, but we are finally figuring out how this changes our views about our country. We are still unable to differentiate between the good people helping and the bad people capitalizing on the death and destruction of others.

Chapter 10
Bet you didn't know

So here we go! Let's begin with the only way we can truly find out what is affecting our lives, and how we can change things to our advantage. Remember, being aware of the many who will try to sway your vote by feeding you many untruths will be in play at all times. The first thing we must do is ignore the riff-raff and think for ourselves.

The first thing we must do is register to vote. If you haven't already, this is a very serious part of having a voice. Registration is not that hard. What seems to be difficult now is when you appear at the polling place, and the crusty old people running the joint will do anything to make sure you have your correct name spelling on your Driver's License and ask for every ID you have. These people are never nice to me. I have never been to a polling place where someone was funny, nice, smiled, or respectful towards me. Never. Some folks will be courteous, but always try to size me up for judgement. Where do they get these precinct workers?

Of course, I do not look like an old lady, and I usually appear in clothing that may not be appreciated by the people sitting there judging me. I have discovered that the way you dress will probably raise eyebrows or will be too youthful for the folks minding the voting store, so remember, be cool. Do not give a hoot what you look like, or how you appear to these people. Having to appear at this activity is one of the first frightening things about doing the voting thing.

We are allowed to be there, and we are allowed to look any way we wish as long as we are "street able" and not naked. Please do not be fooled by the looks or stares from people who feel like they are supposed to be there and you are not. I think that a lot of fear in going to a polling place is how the rest of the people view everyone else coming to vote. Most still think that this is a solemn event like going to a wedding, christening or a funeral. Well, it's not. And don't let others make you feel like you are disrespectful or annoying by just having a smile or dressing in bright or fun attire.

If you have your information pamphlet with you and your sample ballot already marked, the process will take only about 2 or 3 minutes. You will emerge from the little booth with your ballot already to go in the hopper. This part is my biggest concern. Somehow, certain parties have been "losing" ballots, or disallowing the ballot into the security guarded box. I am adamant about receiving a receipt, and an assurance that my ballot was cast properly and the vote would be tallied correctly.

So that's pretty much it, folks. Thank you for reading. Now, I am about to talk to you in regards to what the heck we are voting for and who the heck is getting my vote.

Each time we see a candidate or the candidate's position on a subject which concerns us, we are usually confused. I have heard candidates change their views in one sentence. Now this tactic seems to be one that is inherent to politicians. The fact that each person giving a speech might stray from the written words, and potentially change their minds midstream has happened. I am always hopeful that the changes are for the better and not for the worse. I would believe that I didn't know who would be waiting at the polling place to interrogate me before voting. I felt that way for the longest time. I also didn't know how the task accomplished a winner of the election, without my being able to inspect and be certain my vote would count.

I suppose I also wasn't aware of who gets to be behind the table checking everything identifiable and authorizing a citizen to proceed with the process. I am sure that none of us would have thought that we would be one of the volunteers spending all day babysitting angry voters standing in lines, and being turned away with improper ID. I have no idea how these people get the authorization to make people wait for hours, and create havoc amongst the voters waiting in line.

I think that many of us just assume there will always be a place to vote, people will always be there to man the polling place, and we all will be allowed to cast a ballot with no strings attached. Until the Voters Rights Act was knocked down by SCOTUS. Now gerrymandering is running crazy, and the new game is to disenfranchise the voters any way possible.

Could there be a better way to help others understand what striking down laws that work properly means to the rest of the citizens? Could there be anything which would relieve the nation of the constant lawmakers screwing around with the laws for their profit?

Chapter 11
Do you think critically?

Now is the time to begin to think critically. Each human has the power to process information, become aware of the situation surrounding them, and to follow through on making good decisions. These processes are the basis for each voter to make their voices heard.   But, why do we vote? Why bother contributing to something that is obviously bought and paid for before you even cast your vote?

I think that we vote because we think it matters, yet stand back each election and question the outcome. We have been conditioned to believe many things. The only portion of the democratic experience had faded into a very dark and dirty money scheme that will eventually begin to crumble.

The hopes we, as a country, had started with have been tainted with wealthy and powerful people in control. But this situation has been in existence for a very long time. We have been the slave to a value system that is still not working to sustain life and enhance resources.

We have also been fooled to believe that our whole purpose is to work at jobs we hate, make money to live in the ever-growing population for more cost. How many people have the opportunity to succeed if the value is only money? How many sonatas would have been written, or paintings created if the only prize was money? Is there a way to differentiate between the way we think and the way we should think? I think there is a way to begin the transformation of eliminating the monetary system and begin to heal the planet where we live. I will adhere to a trilogy of documentaries which has changed my life. (Zeitgeist) I will also try to think in the realm of resources and sustaining life as my bottom line.

If we return to the way of the Native Indians, we will have learned that before the existence of money, the humans migrated and lived a very peaceful life. If we return to the cavemen and see that the only purpose of existence was to sustain life, then we can see why our system is delusional. These historic and profound discoveries have been exposed to the evolutionary humans as value. We, as inhabitants currently have not been able to decipher the human needs without incorporating money as a final prize.

There is no doubt that the power derived from the wealth has kept the human population in a state of division. How is it possible for the people with more money to be held in higher esteem than a person without money? How can the potential of every human on this planet to discover or create something that would help the whole human population, kept hindered as a result of being poor? The reason that the separation of wealth and status has perpetuated for thousands of years, and it seems to have flourished and developed into a very dangerous way of living. The monetary system is the biggest and most successful Ponzi scheme of all time. The vanishing revenue and resources are being sold outright to other greedy people so as to make more profit. The free enterprise system is moot. How can we start to change our way of thinking to include the other people on our planet?

Is it true that the wars and resource acquisition has been at the very basis of the world we are living in today? You bet your ass. No doubt the perpetuation of the "need versus want" part of human life is out of control. I think that with this continuous indoctrination upon birth, each one of us is stamped, identified, pre-determined, and put into a pot with the rest of the human numbers. Each one of us born in any country has a mark of birth, numbers, and a paper trail a mile long. All before we are even one-year-old.

Perhaps the only way to change the way we think is to try to cover our tracks going backwards in history. If our goal would be to reach the non-existent wars, and love of the earth we must strive to eliminate all that has made this earth crumble. If the power of money is so great that people kill, steal, borrow, sell, and live for its being, then something is askew.

If the need for learning has to take a step back and observe the results, then this process must happen. If each one of us can remember a time when the money involved was minimal, and the happiness was in the forefront we have already taken a step to healing. Yes, healing. We are all very sick, and the money has perpetuated the living with the illness, without cure. Each dollar printed had no basis and continued to be manufactured out of thin air. There is no more basis for the value of a piece of paper. None of the paper can do anything but burn to keep a person warm. Or to be used to blow one's nose. Valueless.

Chapter 12.
Do we need money?

If we are aware of how to be happy, then how is it possible to do so without having money? If you have had a wonderful meal or sipped a splendid wine, your happiness is human. The very source of the resource is you. Each of us has a level of happiness that makes the world seem brighter and easier to live. Every human has a moment where the laughter is loud, and the squeal of delight is childish. Take that moment and remember that the feeling cannot be bought or sold. The feeling of excitement or thrill is coming from within you. Humans propagate euphoria with a brain syntax that we sought after for our entire lives. Just what makes us so sure that the thing we saw, or the joke we heard wasn't a part of a purchased monetary process? How do we know that the thing that made us laugh wasn't a purchased joke book and passing it off as being created by the teller? It doesn't matter, does it?

You see, the creativity and happiness this joke may have brought to a human's psyche is the only purpose of its creation. I play music because I am so happy to share my talents with others to help them feel the same way I do when I perform the music. Of course, being in the music business and creativity world means no money involved, or rarely involved. So, the continuous devotion to my craft is unable to be valued to anyone but me. The results of my craft are why my motivation is love and feeling, and not money.

Now, each person is working at a job that they hate. Their faces are becoming twisted, and the lives indicate anger and frustration. Their stomachs have lesions, and they are all suffering from slavery. Yes, slavery. The pressure of having to perform a task for a price to be able to exist. Indentured servants to a very serious slave trade that has been set up for profit. Everything that we hold dear to us has been set up for some profit to someone who is not even participating. (Just ask my Agent) It is true that we are all able to sustain our human needs by succumbing to the very people and jobs that make the wealthy scamper higher up the ladder. We remain at the bottom rungs and holding the ladder steady for those who would rather have us dead. Yes, I said they would rather not have just millions of slaves, they would rather have a way to control life itself for the slaves. Thus, no health care, suffering, hunger, murder, extermination, and exposure. I know it seems like some sick game being played on humans, but I do believe this is all out of boredom. If a person has so much money they cannot possibly buy anything else, the psychosis and evil begins. Look at Caligula. He was so bored and sick he began a disgusting and vile process out of sheer boredom. Murder, rape, sodomy, and evil things that people had to witness and while bound by his power and wealth.

No, we have not learned. Why is it that some of us lowly persons of education stand here and watch ridiculous statements, people, situation, and know well we have the power to make this go away? Someone gets up in power who has a price, and easily swayed by a very small percentage of wealthy people. Yes, these powerful and wealthy people are bored. They have no reason to make more money by raping the resources of ours and other countries, they have demented and sick plans to screw with humans. I suppose watching people die, or taking away fundamental human needs is a way to get your kicks if you are bored, but isn't that more of a "spoiled brat" syndrome?

Do we think that our taking control of the monetary system and changing a few parts will help us? Nope. The whole concept of value and resources certainly buried in the brainwashing we received from birth in our country. Heck, pretty much the rest of the world has the same philosophy. Wake up, go to work, make money, and pay the bills, repeat. Where does the happy part come in to play? Why is it that the only times we are happy are on our days off, and vacations or holidays? How can we possibly go through life and only have a few moments to be happy without missing a car payment or getting food on the table?

I answer the questions above by knowing it is not money that makes happiness. Security and sustenance are the secrets. If we are secure in our environment, and the warm, cozy surroundings are familiar, we are happy. If we turn on the water and water comes out, we are happy. If we switch on a light, and it comes on we are happy. If we open the fridge, and there is food inside, we are happy. But are we aware that the water and electricity and sustenance tied to money is why we have a problem?

How can there be a basic right to life on this planet if the water, food, and shelter are being held ransom by wealthy people? You must pay them to have it. Even though, in this century, we can easily put up solar panels and receive electricity. We can drill for water and pump it for free out of the ground. We can grow and create food items for our consumption easily with the land and water. Just how dang lazy are we?

Yes, we are a bunch of lazy consumers. If someone else will make the food, we will buy it. If someone delivers it for a price, we will consume it. The profit from each morsel of food sold is 200%, and your need for prepared or pre-packed food products remains a very lazy way to live a life. Each fast food place visited, each frozen entrée and every soda pop consumed is a major profit to someone else. We pay for the packaging. In every aspect, we pay for advertising, commercials, shipping, without having any idea that we could do this ourselves for virtually nothing. We complain about not having money but insist on spending so much money on convenience we are burying ourselves in addiction.

We all seem to be addicted to something. Shopping, video games, crosswords, food, alcohol, drugs, smoking, and many other things. Perhaps the way we find excitement or satisfaction that equates to something physical. Perhaps not. I know that being addicted and needing something to sustain life are two separate things. Each level of addiction is measured by an action that is physical [breathing] or something that is perpetuated by stimulus [drugs]. We are all prone to an addiction to something, but the need to distort the real world seems to be the basis for a lot of bad addictions. I refer to the bad addictions as things that are human destructive outside provocation. The way the air is tainted, the food products have carcinogens and toxins in them as well as the water with high levels of toxicity.

Maybe it is better to go back to the human body as a temple with caring and nurturing as the origin. If the care of our bodies and the well-being of our endorphins is satisfied, then the living can begin. I think that the majority of we humans understand that we destroy many cells with destructive outside sources. Chemicals and man-made drugs or derivatives have created a very complicated result. People are more disturbed, mentally ill, and the violence or lashing out begins. Had a person been nurtured and attention paid, the illnesses and emotional problems will move towards identification and naturally worked through with one on one assistance. Medications that dilute better or different diets soon replace the senses. People can live with or without medications but if we realize that the chemical inducement of biological healing appears distorted, we can try to use homeopathic or natural sources.

The Natives of many countries have used marijuana, opium, and many other naturally grown medications for multiple cures. We know that opiate derivatives and chemically extracted products from the poppy have been abused and made into an unnatural form. The natural source is less addictive and does a better biodegradable job in a human body. We are aware that the marijuana healing power is great, and the multiple problems in a human psyche or physical problems can be eliminated with its natural form use. We know that the earth has provided many things that are good for the human. We also have extracted many bad things from our earth.

The fossil fuel discoveries and use became the beginning of our demise. The coal and natural gas extraction in our earth's crust has been extensive. The physical earth's destruction to obtain these products has been the sole reason for money. And once again the perpetuation of the wealth factor and money is brought into play. We are so foolish to fall into these traps. The sheep fell right into the trap, and we were conditioned to believe so many things that are not true or real for human life to survive. Must we have cars that burn fuel? Why is it we can build technology to discover other planets, but can't seem to put out sustainable energy? Let me guess.

Chapter 13
I do recommend the *Zeitgeist* Documentaries

After spending a large amount of time trying to understand how the political scene has become so engulfed in money and "The Rapture," I realized that viewing Zeitgeist 2008 and the last Zeitgeist documentary helped me to understand more about the money trails.

I have seen more changes to the way we have been duped into believing money is the only goal we have in our lives. I cannot imagine a musician or an artist who would be using their talents only for the sake of making money. The liberal arts, alone, are just that. Liberal. How is it possible for money to have replaced the feeling of love or while closing one's eyes feeling the wind on our faces?

We were born with no idea what money is. We were only concerned with love, touching, caring, and sustenance. The money part is taught to us, and with our place in society the money determines our self-value. Are you kidding me? How can a person be valued upon birth by only being born into a certain social or monetary circumstance? Oh yes, we are taught this from the very beginning.

The one scientist that may find the cure for cancer, or figure out how to make water from the air could come from a very poor family. There could be someone who isn't even born yet, not completely exempt from using their enormous brain power to help the rest of the world. Why? Because of money. The way that we have moved our human social system to a have and have-not world is pitiful yet alone alarming. Every year that passes, more prices rise, and more people die from illness and poverty. And every year we all stand there and watch without helping to change this process. You see, we can change this, and should hurry up before someone (let me guess who) will control the population of the wealthy countries easily without protest.

We can either take this crap or do something about it. I need to change a few things before I expire, and trying to accumulate more voters with critical thinking skills is my quest.

If one person could understand how our participation keeps the greedy and gerrymandering people out of office, one will finally figure out how to piss off an enormous amount of people without having to expose even our names. We can be discrete and vote our conscience without having to stand up and have a screaming match with ignorant and very uneducated people. We can fight a battle without having to pick up a weapon. And, we can also speak loudly with our voices to help change the pattern of demise.

If we can consider that money is the only way to have an economy, we haven't thought enough about the consequences of having the monetary system. We are not aware of how this money has created a concerning split in human living conditions with the adding of exclusivity to every situation. Keeping people separate from the wealthy people while creating a place of lowliness to anyone who is not with large sums of money.

We know that money is invisible. We are aware of the paper that supposedly replaces its value. But, how can each of us understand what life would be without money? None of us have even given it a thought because the scarcity of certain things in our lives makes the value increase. If we were not able to acquire water without paying for it (which is what the norm appears currently) then the water is valuable somehow. The same can be said for anything physical. If gold is scarce, then gold is valuable. If air is scarce, or water unattainable, we die.

Apparently being human and needing air, water, and sustenance to exist means nothing if you don't add money to the mix. So it goes. Money has risen above food, shelter, plant life, animals, water and food. But we can't eat, drink, or wear money can we?

The information that helped me understand the money thing in our world better, I am thankful for the Zeitgeist Documentaries. Each one has a message that will not only coax critical thinking from our brain but can also help better figure out what we are meant to do while here on this planet.

Every time I see a dollar bill now, I am wondering how many people fought, worked, toiled, enslaved, and received this piece of paper. How many people had touched this precious dollar bill? Was this dollar a part of a scary or evil plot that made the money float to the top? Well, I think that a dollar bill will only have been handled by poor people as the wealthy rarely use cash, and the database that represents money is their play yard.

Yes, the way the money appears to the poorer people is that of being a savior to their many needs. The money will solve all their problems. The money will make all the illness and bad air go away. I am afraid the money will just sit there and do nothing as it always has. We are what makes money valuable. Humans have destroyed the earth to find money, make money, eat and sleep for money. Steal, murder, and hurt others just to have it in our possession. Why? Well, apparently services and goods can be obtained by money. So you need it, right?

Bullshit. We did this to ourselves while blindly following some very wealthy man who thought the "Checks and Balances" method would be perfect for our world. Hundreds of years ago when we could have deleted money existence altogether, we opted to follow this idiot. We did this because someone came along and spoke words we didn't understand, and provided results that meant eating, or having shelter. Buying and selling became the way of the world while the breakdown began without any of us paying attention.

Imagine what life would be like without money. I think nobody can. We have been programmed to think that money is good, and the method in which we value things is just fine. Once again, I am aware that most people are not getting the idea that happiness should always be at the front of the line in needs. I also think that most people understand that money cannot buy happiness, but seems so help replace the rest of the items humans' desire. So basically, a human gets a physical item that distracts from the pain or loneliness. But remember, this is only temporary, and the pain or loneliness will return when the item has lost its usefulness.

We can try to figure out what our world would be like without having to slave and work so as to eat and live. We could wake up every morning and ask ourselves "What wonderful thing shall I do today"? Each one person would more than likely not be able to comprehend a life such as the one without having to fall slave to a value system. Could you go out and enjoy a sunset or stand in a cool lake and expect to be charged money for this? Of course, you know the wealthy are trying to make sure this scenario will come to pass by purchasing all the beauty in the world and charging admission. To have our natural resources stripped for energy use, or to watch the diminishing of the glaciers is the empathy we all feel right now.

In 2015, our desperation is warning railroad systems that their oil tankers may derail, or the local fracking company that their local water sources are capable of being ignited. Somehow the way to achieve a survival instinct and make the best of what is left on this planet is our only recourse. Or is it?

Are we capable of turning things around? Can we by thinking that the way to our life length is by keeping the healthiest of people, air, water, and life sustained at all times?

I am sure that by using critical thinking and weighing the differences in every human's life will be astonishing. I have the optimist view of life, and I wish only to share how wonderful reality is compared to being ignorant in the dark.

.

Chapter 14
Can we do this without money?

So now we know that our demise is money. We understand that no matter where we turn, money will have already been there before us. Someone will have already made millions of dollars on a bridge toll where the bridge paid off its debt more than 50 years ago. The same bridge continues to receive revenues and collects higher and higher tolls for its use. We see that not only do they collect the tolls, but do little to ensure the safety or structural integrity of the bridge. Nope, the big dudes, are pretty quick to forget about that part.

Our country and multiple other countries around the world have been undergoing infrastructure breakdown. The damage to the bridge will eventually create death, catastrophe as well as uncertainty in the people who will cross the bridge. But we still pay to cross the bridge and while in the middle hope that it does not collapse. This is how I feel about the political system in our country. We are all waiting around for things to break to pieces while being sucked into the way the corrupt and money hungry wealthy have controlled us. So far, I am not seeing anything positive coming from this method of governing, and most people agree the system is terribly flawed.

How can we change the way our immediate lives are affected by bad governing? We are aware that if we put people in office who have the same views we do, the result should be a positive and forward moving society. The bad news? Well, each person we seem to put into office turns around and decides to change his views based on the lobbyists purchasing of the officials. The sad news is that we are all aware it is happening and are looking the other way. How are we doing this? By not voting or being complacent in voting the better people into office. We seem to continue to think that the vote we cast will receive rewards somehow. I know I am not one of those people.

Each time I vote for someone, I am fully aware that they may be swayed by some form of influence be it monetary or favor based. Each time I read about the candidates and their views, I am fooled by the sheer nature of the beast. Each politician has a way of making their agenda seem palatable, as well as defining.

If a voting person had a real choice, I mean one where they could truly determine the candidate, we might be better off. I would have enjoyed seeing hundreds of folks run for office with multiple of platforms so as to have a better choice of ideas. Think about how fun it would be to listen to people who thought the same way we do. I would be so very happy to understand I am not alone in the voting booth but feel surrounded by people who accept me for my views and respect each one of my decisions.

We strive to be virtuous and hope that we do not hurt others by the decisions we make every day. We do not wake up, and all of a sudden believe that we as individuals were born to be served by others. This thought makes no sense. I think that each human has a way of connecting with the social world, and others do not. Some people are not interested in having anyone know what they are doing nor are they ready to expose their hearts to others. This is a protective device that all humans have built in. This device is called self-preservation.

We all have the will to live. If we suffocated, the only thing we need is air so that we will not die from asphyxiation. Money doesn't matter, food doesn't matter, and surely nothing else on the planet matters at that moment. The only directive for survival as a biological being is getting air to our lungs and receive oxygen. All wants and desires are cancelled for that duration of time our life is in jeopardy if we do not breathe.

If we are being locked in a cage and starved to death, do we understand why we are being held captive? Is there possibly a way to be able to see how one human can interrupt the flow of living by simply going against that which is instinctive? We must understand that the control and domination over our species make no sense. In the wild, a creature will only dominate over another for territory or food. Perhaps we have been instructed to be continuously competing so as to have more. More food, more space, more control, and more power.

I would believe that we have the power to be able to coexist. Without the continuous effort to "one up" anyone who comes in contact with us. For the sake of the longevity of our species, we must be more diligent in learning how to allow others to achieve. The feeling of power over another seems to be the reason each of us must think more about how to get along without being so dang jealous of each other.

We should probably start from the beginning and try to learn how to survive on our planet with the many obstructions we now have surrounding us.

Chapter 15
The environment is crumbling

It makes sense to think about how people can function with the distractions in our world today all the while performing multiple tasks. Each person who lives on our planet has so many things to do the results can seem convoluted. If we eliminate the value system in an invisible piece of paper which we call money, we can then begin to figure out the path to take. Humans have a basic group of needs that are physiological, emotional, and environmental. The combination of these needs help to guide a human to survival throughout a span of approximately 75-100 years old. Some of our needs are unbalanced and our physical bodies either hold up, or do not.

I am certain that the toxins in our environment also have a great deal to do with how we function. I have noticed that people in areas with cleaner air usually have less medical problems than those in large cities. When remembering the Erin Brockovich movie about water pollution in Hinckley, California, I have begun to attempt ways of eliminating myself from these locations. I would not need someone to try to buy me out of my property, as I would be just fine with leaving on my accord. I think that most people were very stunned when the exposure of toxic waste crossed a line that endangered humans and environment for sustaining life. All for the sake of money.

Thus, the concept of attempting to save the lawmakers from doing more damage to OUR air, water, land, and resources is in order.

We were just sure that voting representatives of the people would provide a group effort in keeping our land and resources sustainable. While we were working hard and not noticing, the lawmakers began the long 50+ year journey of complicating and stalling every law and protection we had on our water and land. We have allowed them to start and maintain fracking; we have allowed them to dump fracking waste into the water sources, and all because of the laws that protect the violators and NOT the humans exposed to this poison. Not to mention the geoengineering with the chem trails and waste disposal in the air.

I do know that the recent and obvious "money for votes" system is blatant and right in front of our faces. We sit complacently and not even attempt to do anything but watch our world shrink smaller and smaller. Most of us are so bothered and frustrated that we want to hide in a cave until it's over. Problem: It's NOT over. And that cave will probably collapse from earthquakes, or fill with water table mixed with fracking toxins, pushed in another direction from fracking, filling the cave with deadly gasses.

No matter how we hide, the facts keep filtering in like a canister of mace breaking up a protest march. We know better, and we still just sit here and complain about the destruction, devastation, and death that corporations are allowed execute.

I should have known when the last Justices of the Supreme Court, who were appointed by Bush, began to come out of their "mole" status and vote out needed laws, and allow corporations to be people. I knew it when the most conservative justices made their move when the Voter's Right's Act repealed in 2013, so they could begin the voting restrictions, legally. The possibilities were endless for the folks who would want you just to "shut up and sit down". (Chris Christie) The people who would wish for the human slaves to give up and do anything the wealthy and powerful folks would desire.

Somehow, I think that this is not the case with most people, and though we attempt to make our voices heard, there are many baffles and barriers that change the level of audio. The possibility of the "last chance of changing the foolish crap" remains with the voting. We are also very aware that the process is in need of changing too.

We must realize that all of the rights we have earned have been taken away by the re-writing of laws. I know that none of us want to have to study law and that we try to leave that to the lawyers but get a clue folks, we need to understand how the law works. Especially on us. We have been catching up on the latest Driving laws, and we take our tests for other businesses to pass and provide services, why can't we just figure out a few other things in the meantime?

Perhaps having a simple life without complication is what we are striving for as a possibility throughout life. But don't you think that living with multiple comparisons of other cultures, geography, art, food, politics, family life, technology, agriculture would create a wonderful basis for perspective!   We think about how we can turn our wasted time into the time to spend with our families, watch a sunset, play with the dog, go for a hike, take a swim, or just have a nice dinner. We do not want to spend hours reading voter's information booklets and try to figure out which lesser evil to choose from when casting a vote.

I always had thought when I walked out of a voter's booth; I would be beaming while saying "I have just spoken, and my voice was heard." Most recently, I have thought that perhaps my registration and time spent for this voting event was for naught. From voter suppression to long lines, the same events seem to keep happening as well as the more difficult the process is becoming.

If the process was made easier in only a few respects, I do believe people would be participating more. Some of we older folks remember when it was a big event to go out and vote. We could make the visit to the polling place a family thing, and have dinner afterward. The groups would go over after church and participate, with a warm feeling of "belonging" in the air. What the heck happened? How was it easier to feel the love and companionship of the country with the same people every year, and all of a sudden lose each and every Right one after one? I know that we have added a few technology aspects to the distraction we have undergone, but I also know that the way to notice the changes is to look up from the phone, computer or television set and pay attention to the life that is passing by faster and faster.

Maybe we need to pay attention to the money flow... the money is what is killing our planet as well as the gluttonous resource monsters sucking the life out of our planet.

Bitchfest aside, I am sure that the majority of us out here in the real world are ready to explode soon with frustration and helplessness. But I remain inclined to complain. In hopes that the people who will read about the voting propaganda and the way, voting has been "modified" to suit the people with the most money. Money is the problem, money is the basis, and money has created no value to human or life on our planet.

The way to appeal to people who do not vote is so complicated currently. In 2015 with the elections coming up, our view of how the candidates line up and try to explain their positions begins to confuse people. The people have such a hard time understanding the "real" views because the candidates are burying the truth under piles of statistics that their staff has created out of thin air. Each time the next candidate stands in front of rich, white people their words are racist and bigoted. Then, they stand in front of multi-racial crowds and profess equality. All the while the voters who excluded from participation seem to be the very same masses who would be putting the politician into office.

Doesn't this seem rather ridiculous? We are all aware of their backgrounds, and yet they will continue to frighten us with "foreign threats" and baffle us with the political banter that none of us understand. How do we define their façade and expose the lies that they cling to, hopelessly?

I do believe that the way to achieve a common voice is to expand on the issues that have to do with ourselves, first. We can work our way outward as we progress through the knowledge of voting.

Chapter 16.
Guess I need a law degree to vote

The Electoral College is obsolete. Even the concept of how we are still keeping the voting structure from so long ago, intact is foolish. I understand what the concept was when first enacted, but what the heck?

We know for a fact the process was conceived to get the voting results from miles apart and people who were separated by distance to the final tally. We also know that the process helped to ensure the local and rural areas would be exemplified properly with a representative.

OK, that was in the late 1700s, and there was no technology to get the election results to the newspapers and big cities. Before modern technology, this era was not the time where the use of telegraph or telephone for delivering the winners of elections as final. The Electoral College exists solely so as to have the tally done locally and the delivery of the results to Washington faster. Fast forward to 2015 and we are getting a little confused as to why there is not a popular vote, period. Really? One vote for who we want. Very simple. This method would not only save time but certainly make the outcome extremely simple to understand. It is very hard to comprehend how a vast majority of people want a candidate, but the other guy gets elected because of the state's delegates because they can change their minds. That makes no sense and is NOT totally functional in our society.

Perhaps the idea would have made sense when there were only a few hundred thousand people in the USA, and the distance between towns, homes, and areas were just too complicated in the voting process, but to eliminate the people by herding them together in one pile? I think not.

It makes more sense to change the rules and laws to accommodate the millennium. We have no chance of progressing with the same institutions that are destroying the forward progress. The monetary system is foolish. The money has no resources to back it up. If we are so blind that we cannot see the diminishing value (which we used to base on precious metals) of the piece of paper we call money.

The Electoral College had a function and had not allowed the country to progress with the technology as a basis for 200 years. Yes, I do think it is about time to update the way we do business around here. We remember in our Civics classes that the election process is a certain way, and yadda-yadda, but there is not a point to continuing throughout life with very foolish methods of guiding our country. We are already aware of the corruption, greed, criminal activity, and monster behavior. I for one am very happy to use current technology to make voting easier and more verifiable.

We have been trained to fear and respect whatever method that arrives in our laps for consideration. No questions asked. All of us are totally cognizant of the foolish procedures with the way we vote, and starting with the people who run all the way to the way the election outcome is determined needs repair work.

Sometimes the confusion of how our system operates perpetuates the voter to ignore the civic duty. Yes, I said civic duty. Like serving on a Jury. It makes sense because all of us are using multiple services, and if we want people to participate in life, there must be a service that could incorporate all the wonderful and diverse skills we all possess. Most people are very stingy with their talents, and the current protection of talent and services keep falling back on money. How valuable you are, what you provide, how long is taken, and what resources you bring with you to the table. This bag supplies that we provide daily is being taken advantage of by people who are reaping all of the benefits from the labor.

We are caught up in how much we are worth instead of how much we can assist life to sustain itself for our pleasure and longevity. The possibility of our citizens having any say in an election begins with participation. Because of the way we have been taught to participate, the ominous task of making decisions with critical thinking used to be the sole purpose of voting. Oh, my have things changed from when I first voted in 1972 to 2015.

I recall the changing while Nixon was in office, and with the passing along of the "hidden laws" then came the many ways our monetary system maintains total manipulation this day. The introduction of trickle-down economics and Reagan introduced our country to a whole new group of people who finally executed the longest fought battle of obtaining all of the wealth in history. Thus, the remainder of our new generations became confused and complacent in trying to correct the many mistakes that took over the way our banking system and government subsidies systems worked. Every time a debt occurred in our country, the process would be to cut the most fundamental and lowest denominating classes with the assistance in healthcare, nutrition, welfare, and education.

Each time another vote is cast in an election, the old protection is disappearing, and nothing is left in its place. There would be nothing left to place a safety net under our citizens, and the human slavery will increase to massive proportions. Oh wait, this has already happened. We are living a foolish election system, and still trying to tell our people that it "matters" when we vote. We are all fooled every time. At this point in the election process, we ARE NOT the least bit a contributor to the laws that are passing. The lawyers, judges, and enforcement agencies are in total control of our society. The topper is the money that propels them to do the things we are finally able to see.

Even if a law passes the ways the legislature reads, the law will be challenged and will not have to be upheld because it will be in litigation. Now that seems very foolish. The law should be enacted and followed until otherwise proven unnecessary by repeal or change. At this point in the life of a law, the judges and lawyers chime in. I would have thought that perhaps the people who are elected could be from all walks of life so as to be able to represent all views and types of folks.

We currently have, as the majority of our representation, lawyers. Every one of our politicians involves themselves in the determination of law. Do we realize that this fact is not as it used to be? We are currently not represented by farmers, property owners, ranchers, store owners, and common folks. Our laws are written in ways so as to complicate or confuse the reader. The laws take lawyers to figure out the contents while people were being sent away to prison for their color or social status while not breaking any laws. Insane judgements, crazy sentences, and complete injustice are paraded right in front of our eyes. I truly believe that a simplification of the laws, and the ease of information written in a language where everyone with a USA public education can understand.

We write the voting provisions and laws the same way. I think it is equivalent to the tests given to obtain a driver's license. The questions are written so as to be an opposite answer, and confuses people. The past has shown us that the more complicated the words, the easier it is to sway a voter to believe they have made the right choice. Once again common sense and critical thinking would be a very good talent to possess when voting.

Sometimes the media gets it right. Some good channels will allow documentaries and other alternate sources of information to infiltrate their very biased broadcasting. We can try to see other people's views, but sometimes the people are so wrong and the facts so skewed large amounts of patience in watching is needed. If the people are paying more attention to the message and who is sponsoring the advertisements (small print in the corner.) then we can do the research and see who is telling the truth.

Chapter 17
Ideas are resources

We have taken a look at the reasons why we should change the voting methods. I am certain that the ways that people live have changed over the years, so perhaps the only way to view the new millennium is how each person can contribute with their "say" in the governing. I know we think that the wealthy will just buy up the votes but think about the number of wealthy people versus the general population. We also know that they "pitchfork" and "protest" method works. Yes, it works. Nothing like watching a very small amount of Richie Rich scamper into a hole and hide from the masses.

I could elaborate on my squeals of delight thinking that possibly I would be able to witness the "taking down of the statues" erected to commemorate the truly despicable. We have the need to eliminate the bad symbols of our country and start to replace them with honorable and dedicated effects. The Nazi flag was removed from the social exposure to be replaced, recently, with a Confederate battle flag. So, does that not seem less likely to honor evil people as well? And why is it we happen to need a flag? Are we talking about the imaginary borders we have drawn on our planet, lines that we fight and kill over? Lines that determine whether we can be happy, free, or empowered? This concept of flag waving and patriotism is rather unfamiliar in the general species evolution and migration planet where we live.

People have created the lines and have made it impossible to thrive as a species because by putting a "value" in the form of an invisible basis, we are sucked into a very deep hole of deceit and fraud. The aspect of being a part of the world, and yet trying to feel a part of our country is becoming skewed. We have stopped including the earth in our endeavors and have begun to destroy the very thing that sustains our life. We have done this all for the sake of money.

The greed involved in this is at the root, by our feeding into the lie with our personal self-interest at heart. Nobody seems to remember that the need for "things" is a manufactured high. We only can take the pill, get a buzz, then we come down when the effects have worn off. I presume the folks who are drinking and numbing themselves have already had enough of the crazy slave work life and are ready to bid the physical earth farewell. We also have become more aware of how this whole lie and fraud continues to destroy, and why.

When the folks from the past were foolish enough to succumb to the wealthy or well-off people, the slave domination began. All people "wanted" more and more. The desire to have something that nobody else had been running amuck. We began to steal, and harm people to get what they have. If we could not afford something ourselves, we would spend a long time trying to figure a way to get it. No matter what we would have to do, we would still "want" for more. Every child loves their favorite toy, but will "want" another one if they see it on television, as well as any person who is caught up in material belongings.

With each human born comes a helpless phase where the adult must physically care for them. Teaching the younger humans the ways of, the older human's past experiences seems to generate love and compassion. All of the teachings of their past experiences will be passed down to the younger generation of humans. The learning can be a lifetime in the process. The life a human could live would be long, fruitful, and fulfilled if they have food, water, air, and elements to sustain themselves. I think that the learning stages are easily applied to our governing and voting process as well.

We can watch our methods evolve and gather strength in truth. We can see each new day as hope for a happy experience with a full day's involvement. We could help others, and fee needed then take care of ourselves with the joyful company, wonderful food, and a beautiful sunset. All of which we could just experience, without having to buy it, receive credit for it, or have it handed to us with strings attached. Our perspective on the space we take on this planet is sacred to many without our being aware of how our actions affect others.

Don't we think we can make a change by speaking up? I am hoping that the people who have been oppressed and held down enough to come finally forward and want to march or register to vote. I am hoping that the same people are not afraid to stand up for what will affect them and their families. With the way, we attempt to live our lives while the wealthy are sucking us dry is commendable and forthright. The way each one person has special talents or skills can assist the rest of the citizens who are unable to speak out.

I am hoping that the place we live will be forever providing resources because we humans bothered to make sure we were not raping the planet's resources without replacement. I am very hopeful that our people will have the technology and ideas regularly coming so that we can provide for the starving planet, as well as become more contributory to the needs of life.

Chapter 18
Voting, participation, and human worth

So the people who are not interested in voting are the same people who will be very happy to indulge in a political conversation or thrust their views on others. I know that more times than I would want, people have been very quick to voice their political views without ever having voted. Or perhaps they might have voted a couple of times, but find that the information packages and complications in providing information seem ominous to them. I would imagine the person standing in front of a polling booth and being nervous about entering. The process seems hard, but the hardest part is the fact that voting is truly a crap shoot.

We haven't quite gotten ahold of the liars, cheaters, and greedy asses who are making the whole process a laughing stock. The rest of the world is snickering, and I know by being a person who tours the world that our country has pretty much lost a load of respect from the globe. All voting in our country is bullshit. Yes… it's true. It is manure, poop, crap, or whatever you want to call it. We have allowed the most bigoted and racist white rich people to manipulate the Supreme Court, change the laws to allow Citizens United to dominate the funding of candidates, Corporations are now People, Voters rights Act ended, and the pressure to quash anyone who is not wealthy remains a final goal. Then what? Slavery again?

I think that the bitchfest is starting now. I am about to show the selfish, who cannot spend a moment without challenging the majority of the citizens of our country, who's boss. Every person who can speak up or say their piece is needed. We can join and create solidarity with those who are in need to vote. We can help people get registered, or drive them to get their ID. We can all look around and see that the conservatives have moved so far to the extreme right that their ideas and comments are not based on anything alive in this nation but rich white men.

No women are included in rights, no people of color, no children, no poor people, and especially no seniors who are not rich. There is nothing left but rich, white men. So, perhaps they are happy with that amount of human lives left on the planet, but somehow I do not see any of these people cleaning their houses, or giving birth, or growing their food, or fixing their cars. Somehow, the rest of the population has a purpose. The difference is, how do we make sure the result is not being in servitude or slavery to someone else?

Obviously, the direction the extreme conservatives are headed is not the same way we are headed. And as a woman and a musician, I am aware that [they] don't like me at all. I am certain the right would be very happy to eliminate me, and all my liberal friends. They would be happy to execute literally and torture anyone who is not white, male, and rich. The concept that these people are interested in controlling, inflicting torture and pain, shooting, hunting, oppressing, starving, and allowing us to die from illness is the basis for their existence. I am certain that the people who are in "control" have such a huge plan for the middle and lower class folks, we cannot fathom the evil and sloth they are indulging.

The voting by the people of our country was supposed to help all citizens have a voice. The founding fathers had predicted many things could come from the laws and rights that our country was trying to abide. We realized that we had to change and amend certain laws so as to keep the present intact. We all needed to remember that our human population and the eras in which we have gone through certainly marked change in our society. I also believe that the gathering of the people in masses will eventually prevail in anything that oppresses our populations.

It is in our nature to end up at the marker where the human instinct takes over from the imaginary borders or human value. Just how much is a human worth nowadays? Did anyone ever think that we have been valuing people all along, and even though we had fought a war to stop the enslavement of humans, the humans continue to be enslaved?

We have come to the point where either the humans will be forced to comply with the "Masters" or have a revolution and remind the population that these "Masters" are only few in numbers. Groups in large numbers have always ruled the earth. The possibility that the leaders of groups are something other than just another human being is the issue. Somehow these people have separated themselves from the rest of us, and decided that they are "magical"? How does it make any sense to see people who hold themselves above others for reasons that are non-existent? How do we keep falling for all of this crap?

I think that the only thing the controlling few have going for them is that they can still use the money to buy people. Which brings me back to my question: Just how much is a human worth nowadays? Can someone come up with a dollar amount? And, if the person being evaluated for worth has special traits or skills are they more valuable in money?

Perhaps the idea that people have no other way to express themselves unless they can brag about what they "have." Most folks will always want more. No matter where a person sits in his or her living room, they would change and add to the contents. Each time we drive through a community and glance to houses and property, we see things we would like to "have." Of course, every little boy and girl see things on TV that they "want" desperately so as to throw a tantrum if not appeased. I think that maybe we are all this way. Maybe we all would lay down on the floor and scream if we cannot get the one thing that would make our life complete if we "had" it.

I am fully aware that the people on this planet all have a different sense of needs and wants. I also know that the environment in which a person lives is also a contributing factor to how a human will be able to survive. We know that the planet is finite. We also know that we can replenish resources, maintain the earth's provisions so as to keep life evolving. So, what happened? Did something change where humans stopped worrying about where fresh water will come from, or food sources? Did the human race decide that we had plenty of resources in large quantities, so we could go on forever? Oops. Not the case. The earth is finite, if we don't take care of what we have left, we will die off. All because of something that is imaginary and based on debt.

Money can have multiple meanings to different people. I am aware of how each person has placed their value on money. Money can mean safety, luxury, peace of mind, future needs met, as well as confidence in surviving. Now, how did this definition and many others pertain to the current explosion of wealth gaps and poverty in our world? Why would the amount of people who own everything on the planet only calculate to 80? 310 Billion People own squat. Something is truly wrong about how this money thing is going. The banks and wealthy own everyone and everything. They have even discovered how to own the water and sun so as to deprive or replenish humans and animals at their whims.

To my recollection, I do not remember how the Indians could have possibly had this type of theory in their lives. I do not know who could have possibly taken the sun and hidden it away so that nobody could use its rays.
I remember a movie with Cheech Marin where they had been a recluse for 20 years from the 60's

and came back to society to see how things developed while they were away in their commune. One of his friends had opened a tanning salon and was doing well in business. Cheech had thought this to be very strange and asked, "Hey man, how did you get the sun to shine just on your place?" The same thing occurs to me when I think of the wealthy confiscating the natural resources and making us all pay to have anything the earth has to offer. This method is insane, and we are all foolish for allowing this to happen.

Chapter 19
Gee, I wonder what is making this hard for us.

I remain concerned about the monetary system. I know that the way we can change how the earth and resources are preserved, shared, and guaranteed depends on us. We humans have destroyed so much of the bounty the earth has given to live. Life is not only people but all things. We seem to forget how the same people who preserved our planet before the greed and corruption kicked in because of money. Money has done more damage on our planet than any storm, earthquake, or Tsunami.

So here we sit. Doing nothing. Taking more and more from our earth, and paying more for what he are rationed by the "Masters". How did people acquire natural resources and replenish them in the past? I remember many stories about the Indians who would make sure they gave back to the earth from what they took. It is understood that the people who were not living in a civilization based upon money would survive and flourish. The reason for success would be how they lived off the resources provided to them. They evolved common farming into a new and more streamlined way to not damage the earth and to rotate crops so as to help the soil. These things were learned and by trial and error.

I presume we are all aware of the way the earth and the waters which are fresh versus salt have their own intricate system which cannot be manipulated. Yet, somehow humans have done so much damage to the earth surface, the earth may not have any way to recover. How can we change back something that has become extinct? There is a reason why we have that word, "Extinct". We have done this already, so we had to name it.

All for the sake of money. Killing, stealing, corruption, material items, luxury, raping, controlling, oppressing, torturing, murdering life, and living creatures. How do we define the insanity versus psychosis or social norm? How did killing and murder become a part of our lives on a daily basis without our batting an eye?

The obvious answer is money and power. I took a class at University in Political Science called "Wealth and Power in America". Not only had we learned what each facet of the global governments, but we had also learned what each definition meant. We had to put this information into perspective and realize that the whole world had taken portions of government "types", and created their own for their separate situations. The information that I had obtained from the study of how each definition continues to include the same needs by each country. I began to realize that all of the "types" of governments in the world had been derived from the previous methods. Each country had a certain provision which only included the particular country of government.

Now the question is, how do we know which type of government works?

I hear multiple uses of the words "Fascism, Stalinism, Communism, Monarchy, Marxism, Oligarchy, Plutocracy, Socialism, Theocracy, Dictatorships, and Maoism, etc. Sheesh people... I am so tired of "isms" and trying to differentiate between the best and the not so good ways to "herd people" is insane. Well, more futile than insane, because the same little factor keeps popping up. The same reason why people are separating their own kind from each other. Gee, I wonder what that is.

The apparent point to value and money keeps rearing its ugly head so as to distract anyone who has "wants". The value of "having" things and wanting more is the common method in 2015. I am certain that the money and wealth have propelled the gluttonous and greedy human brain to strive for more and more. But for what? To "have" more than the next guy? I am wondering if we have ever heard the phrase "You can't take it with you" before? How is the purpose of living on this beautiful planet changed to what materialistic crap we can "have"? The only and certain thing we know in our world is death. We know this all of our lives. We know this is inevitable. There will never be a change to the destiny of the human physiology. We will all die. So the fact that we stand here and deny that the "isms" may have some sort of basis to a well-run government system is foolish. We cannot possibly be so ignorant to think that Democracy is the only way to help millions of people without fixing a few things to eliminate the money games. Apparently the whole government systems have strayed from the prosperity of the country to the wealth of the country. These items are separate. Prosperity is also the human happiness and well-being factor. A country who prospers is providing the world with things that they are proud of. The craftsmanship of different civilizations is still diverse and thrilling to observe. I know that the money trail leads to the sources of wealth, but who is manipulating the natural order of things for mankind because of the money alone.

The money trail always leads to those who disregard the only thing a human can know about the future. We, as humans only know ONE THING for certain in our lives. We know that we will die. No matter what amount of money is given to us, no matter what wealth we possess, no matter what stuff we have, the cost of death is still undetermined. The reason there cannot be a value on life is because the human life is valued differently by separate entities. How do we know how much a human is worth if the only thing equivalent is "imaginary money"?

The whole world's monetary system is based upon debt, and that has been a certainty which was created to manipulate humans. The money trail will also lead to the basic reasons for all human behavior in this day and age.

The reason why we have robberies is to steal money. The multiple reasons why people are killed is because of money, drugs; money, power; money, manipulation of people; money; fraud; money, theft; money, and the reasons why the value of life is completely askew is because of money. So, we have been made aware that we screwed up. We allowed the world to fall into the checks and balance system, copying the European methods, and still are being manipulated by their system. We have been sucked into the same system which promised people would be able to share, and then changed their minds.

Look, this problem is ongoing. The best and finest scholars have tried to warn us for centuries. We have ignored the warnings and jumped straight into the fire. The banking system and monetary system on our planet is foolish and has no basis for survival by human life. Nor will the animal, vegetation, and water system survive.

So here we sit with our lives going down the tube and none of us are even worried. We seem to be distressed about the rent, gas for our cars, and food for our families with only attention being paid to how we can get more money to survive. Wouldn't you think it funny that the Indians, in the years BEFORE we stole their lands and killed their indigenous people, would have been concerned with money or "collateral value"?

I know and so do all the readers out there that the joke is on us. We did this to ourselves while thinking that we would be "like the rich people, or the haves" by just working and slaving to obtain money. The value system is so off kilter that our entire lives revolve around work slavery and complete obliviousness to the power who holds us at one place in society. There will be no progression or evolution by natural means. There will be nothing to do in a lifetime without being evaluated for worth. Perhaps the value in human innovation and ideas have been lost to those who would be jealous. Some people are intimidated by those who are creative, artistic, and think from the "art and design" side of the brain. You see, we all think from different sides of our brains. We cannot all be the same. So the folks who are mindless or uncreative will strive to be vengeful so as to remove the excitement from anyone else.

Chapter 20
Now we know why we must vote

The voting process was designed to allow the people to help govern themselves. OK, well that worked for a week or two, then the amendments began. Our constitution has been ratified, amended, changed, added Bill of Rights, and determined multiple laws to help our country manage a population. Well, if the process was the least bit easy to understand, the lawmakers have decided to make sure the common person in our country have no way of understanding what the laws say. Thus, the need for the group of people called "Lawyers". The manipulation of the law and how it pertains to the citizens is their job. The way a person can commit murder and walk away Scott-free becomes their directive with no consideration to being fair to the people or victims in the process.

We are very aware of the way our prison system is all "for profit" which indicates that the process for a person to end up in a prison is also being bought and paid for. So if the crime is committed by someone with money (or white), the lawyer is paid, the witnesses compensated, the arresting officer is ignored, the judge is swayed, the facts are lies, and the criminal walks away from the whole process only to commit the same crimes over and over. Or the other way around if the suspect is unable to afford an attorney, is black or a darker color. The criminal is railroaded, arresting officer unjustified (or will have shot the suspect without cause), the judge is swayed, the lawyer is paid by the state/feds, the witnesses are non-existent, the crime is minor, but the suspect goes to prison for 30 years.

So how does this process assist anyone in our country? How is it possible for the same people who commit crimes while white or rich to not punish the same way as we regular folks? I do not recall reading laws and seeing the specifications regarding which citizen has rights or which does not. The way I read it is, "WE THE PEOPLE". Nothing was mentioned about the color, race, or creed of the "people". Nobody said anything about the wealthy or prominent stature in the community which would allow the rules to be different. I didn't read one word about the wealthy and white males (slave owners) who created this country mentioning anything about who the "people" are in specific format.

To be able to vote is something that we citizens are forgetting. Over and over we continue to bitch about the ways which seem ridiculous in our generation. We have been complacent in making the path easier for our children. We have been very foolish to have allowed the wealthy and greedy people to make the laws which exempt them from the way we must live our lives. How do these laws get passed and how did we miss the subtle changes which have changed our entire lifestyle? How did we all miss the ways the governing bodies have secretly changed the ways we are governed, and they have been excluded from the process? I know that the questions are many and the answers are few. I also am aware that the way we have allowed this to happen to us is and will always be our own fault.

But that does not make each of us unable to change this. We can wallow in the self-pity of the results of the unjust laws or we can do something to change the laws. We need to remember the people we put into these positions are unable to think about the citizens once they arrive at the final destination of power. Each of these people is also unable to determine which law relates to their constituents. We need more people who cannot be bought or sold.

Every time a person squashes a smaller person, the power becomes increased. The powerful become manipulated by the even more wealthy and powerful. The lawyers, judges, police officers and city government have their own agenda, and it does not include anyone else but the same cast of characters.

The reasons why the government seems to be crunching down upon us is because the militarization and supplying the police with military-style weapons. I cannot imagine a life in our country with the constant view of a "prison type" security detail in a tower watching each person. I would tend to believe the amount of security would have to be immense to be able to control millions and millions of people. How could that be done? I have heard the crap about the Nazis and that our country could end up like Germany. You have got to be kidding me. Germany was the size of Oregon. I would tend to believe that the amount of space and people involved would be very easy to control. But we are talking about a country that is 50 times the size of Germany, with millions more people. The process would be so daunting, the government could not possibly round up all the rednecks with weapons, or even find half our population.

So, the control freaks are doing something else to control our population. Destroying the water sources, eliminating the food sources with chemicals, destroying the breathable air, and messing with the lives of millions without having to lift a weapon. Pretty clever, eh?

<u>So now we know why we must vote.</u> We have an obligation to the planet. Only we, the people, can create a better place without the destruction of the very resources we need to survive. The people in government positions are not all terrible people. There are some folks who have been fighting for years to stop the greedy, loathsome congress from destroying even more people's lives with death, poverty, illness, starvation, and no education.

Chapter 21
Let's try to figure out what to do next

More people are going off the grid than ever in 2015. I have heard stories of people moving out of large communities to hide in the backwoods or mountains to escape the constant vacuum of money. Some people have been doing this for years and have a very good idea as to how to eliminate the official's "breathing down our necks" games. I can only hope that the rest of us pay attention and try to understand why this process of escape has been a solution as opposed to sticking out the madness.

I know a few people who had moved to a very lovely little piece of property in the mountains, against a nice stream which ran all year round. Initially, when they bought the piece, they tried to see how to hook up the utilities as the location was very far away from the utility district. The amount of money they would have had to pay for the electricity alone was something like 28,000 dollars, and this amount would be charged to the homeowner.

When my friends opted to not have the service hooked up, and thought about just using the solar panels for electricity, they received a letter from the county telling them they could not live in this place without being hooked up to the utility district.

We all laughed because they had no way of justifying this letter, nor did any law state the possibility of being penalized for using the sun. How could someone just decide that an alternate method of energy was against the law? I have also heard of New Mexico and Arizona thinking about charging people for putting up solar panels a fee and a continuous billing for using the meter on their homes. They will fly and drive around and look at homes that have panels on them and send them billing to get their cut from the sun's rays. The utility people do not want a home to generate power back into the grid because that is what their job pertains to, and they receive revenues for this business.

I realized that most utility districts have no laws which state that you cannot put a well in or use a solar panel on your home. Not yet anyway. I am also certain that the folks who have already done the process are being mocked, or harassed by the utility companies. Each and every company will attempt to make sure a citizen in our country is attached to them for resources needed to survive. You know this is the plan. And it is working quite nicely, I would say.

Doesn't this process seem to be dominating how the energy is being disbursed in our country and around the world? The same way the money has driven the resources to include the sun and the natural water sources, we have fallen for the utility system.

I would have thought the people in charge of delivering the water through expensive pipes and canals could listen to the people for a change. We would like to have clean drinking water. It's pretty simple. The request is marred by the continuous lawmaking which allows more and more toxins to be poured into waterways. And they still charge us enormous prices for this water. How can this be? How is it possible for people to stand there and watch the river become more and more polluted without doing anything?

All of the people on this planet have become lazy. We have just resigned ourselves to accepting such horrible changes to our planet. None of us have the way to repair such a finite resource elimination, and our replenishment process is non-existent. The Indians had a method of replacing all that they took from the land. The earth is and was always the provider of the life we all needed to survive. I am appalled and dumbstruck when I see the continuance of the destructive nature in my midst.

I would also presume that since our country is so foolish, the only way to see the possible finality to our resources is to have them vanish. I know that the "proof" is sad for millions who will die and suffer from the continuous obstacles in the way of healthy living. The Big Pharmaceutical companies, the Big Oil, Utility companies with Nuclear power, and the massive manufacturing processes throughout the world spewing toxins into the air and land are totally responsible.

And we sit here. Speaking what we know as the truth, without being able to do anything about the problems. We were taught that we could elect people who would represent our needs as communities. We were told that the people would fight for their constituents and help those in larger numbers. They informed us that we were able to vote and have our voices heard. Each politician spoke to every one of us and looked in our eyes and lied. The "spinning" is out of control, and the lies are dominating the meager minded in the voting process.

Is it possible to think that perhaps being more educated about voting could help? I am certain of it. Proven facts and gathered information regarding issues which pertain to ourselves should begin the process. We should be able to come to a reasonable and defined result in our research to choose the correct representative for our interests. But something happens in the process of the very easy and simple ways to know your voting methods, and use them wisely.

First of all, we must learn to make the voting process fun or exciting enough to participate. The reason people are not interested in voting is because of the blood baths and serious death threats to those who would think differently than you on an issue. Each time a law is passed and it affects us we freak out. Yet, the same people who are so verbal about injustice are usually those who do not participate until after the fact. We are all on a delayed reaction basis in our country. We seem to wait until things happen that are so horrific until we decide that perhaps this is incorrect behavior or occurrences. Is this the way we want to keep doing this? Are we certain that each one of our interests are even being considered when the "big boys" are voting up on the hill? Well, you have better believe that NONE of us are any consideration to the foolish folks running a Clown Congress and playing games with our lives.

We would all be better off just ignoring the politicians and forgetting the way they have changed laws to only affect the wealthy in a positive way. None of we citizens are in the loop as to how anything voted in government has anything to do with us. We are not a consideration when they are polluting the water or fracking the land around us. They are not concerned when the veterans are dying on the streets after fighting in wars created by the GOP to obtain more wealth for the Big Oil and Energy Kings out there. We are also pretty aware of how they are raping every tree and resource we have left in our country, and all over the world while diminishing the Rain Forest and sucking the seafood out of the oceans. Nothing will be left for future generations to eat, drink, or live upon if these people have their reign for any longer.

We must do something soon (Now!) or we will certainly regret the chance we had to change things. I know that the process seems very complicated, and not voting shouldn't be an issue, but somehow it has become the only way, apart from the pitchforks, to get some attention.

If we have the time to play video games, or a moment to check out a favorite television show, I know we can fit a process like voting into our schedules. I also am certain that the people who will change our world are those with ideas and are creative in their thinking. These people will be our saviors and will be able to increase technology to where the certainty of dependency on a government, utility, or medical assistance will be gone. There will be no people to become the "middleman" in the operation.   The sun shines on my house, and I catch the rays. No fuss, no muss. No intrusion from the government, nor one utility company sticking their greedy hands out for a cut of something that is FREE and is available to all who would participate.

Chapter 22
How the heck to make voting fun?

Well, we know that we play fantasy football, and become excited when we see the dream team's we have put together. Or perhaps we have seen what outstanding fashion team has created out fall fashion trends for the year and we are thrilled to see the new clothing coming down the runway.

I have created many games and things to do while I am driving long distances or having to entertain kids in a car. I think that we are certainly able to come up with a better and more pleasurable way to vote in our elections. I could think about how I would create a "dream team" in the governing methods and the views which include me. I should think that the party affiliations should not be placed on the candidate. I also believe that we can better differentiate between candidates if we remove their labels. The possibilities of stripping the generalization on each person running could help in all of our decision when we vote.

Wouldn't it be nice if we could create the leaders and their teams to represent the people like the founding fathers had hoped upon signing the

Declaration of Independence? We had hoped that we could show the world how to democratically govern itself with the aid of trust and honor. Oops. So far the governing of ourselves has turned into a money race to see who can be bought and sold first. Or more so, whoever has the most money, wins.

We have changed our thought that people are valuable for their skills and contributions to the general society in which all of us live. The United States has been a super influence on the rest of the world in trends, technology, and creativity but has slowed down due to our consumerism.

Yes, we have changed the way we live to allow the insane imbalance of wealth as well as changing the complete demeanor of how people function among others. Somehow changing to exempt the natural order of things is rather defeatist. In all aspects of human and life sustenance, the special gift that is given by those who take resources is to replace what you take. I know the Indians and many others had that mindset and conducted their civilization accordingly.

We could make the politicians into cartoon characters and possibly look at their images with more tolerance. Most of the politicians are the same geeks who have a very hard time with presenting themselves to a general population. Most are so hideous looking and act so disdainfully, they are already characters. Take Donald Trump for example. The man is a very strange version of what he might have thought he looked or acted like when he was 30 years younger. The persona has morphed into a very strange looking older man, with a yellow dyed comb-over, and a mouth that looks like a bellybutton.

Is this what we are coming to? Only looking at a candidate and deciding that we do or don't like them doesn't make much sense. And here we are, the judges of the "fashion candidate" while calling Hillary's pantsuits mundane, and spending more time bashing her hairdo. Nobody can say a word about her experience, knowledge or aptitude. Just the pantsuits.

Or perhaps the fact that people in the political sphere seem to think of themselves as "bigger than life". Some candidates have changed their looks to adapt to the way people need to see them. Are we so foolish that we do judge a book by its cover? So now might be the time when we need to change our way of looking at these freaks. Yes, these people are NOT normal. They all have a need to be a leader. Each one of these people sees themselves being worshiped and hated at the same time. It's like the plantation owner who is happy to see his "flock" of slaves, sheep, cows, pigs, and farmland who all detest him.

I am sickened by the way people have not participated in our natural "order of things" changes. The Constitution was written so as to be amended, changed, and laws enacted to keep up with the changing times. So now we need to think about what might make us happy while doing our civic duty and voting. I think we could make this process a little easier and probably change a few more thoughts about how voting means nothing anymore.

If we think about the procedure as a scary or nerve-racking ordeal, the way our minds react is to feel repulsion, anger, and animosity for those who would want you to participate. I understand that most people are not able to grasp the voting practice. I also think that a fun game could be created to make the whole voting process easier to swallow.

Chapter 23
So here's what I suggest

Voting in numbers is the secret. Turning the studying and understanding of the voter's information pamphlets into a night out (or in) with friends or family while figuring out what or who to vote for. Each time I open a voter's info book, I am stunned by how the same dribble is on page after page. Each biography or information on every candidate reads like a brochure for a travel trip.

I have often wondered who is responsible for determining the text on each person. I note that the information is usually about their voting records, and include a few boring facts about their childhood. None of this information means a thing to me. I not only do not care where they were raised, I am more aware of the actions of their governing experience or how much they have learned after leaving the "grew up in" place. Is it relevant to me that they were born and raised in a state which they are running? I really do not care, because the past has nothing to do with the current events, and their childhood would have been changed dramatically as time moved on. Each person has a basis. Each candidate will try to either distract a voter from the secret agenda they have been paid for or at least lie to the constituents so as to not perpetuate their genuine belief. I think this is where we all get nauseous.

I think that most people would truly enjoy something tedious or monotonous changed into a fun time. If anything, an interesting time. I have decided to think about the voter's pamphlets as a basic guide to the NAMES only. Political affiliations are dividing up the information and coaxing people to generalize the categories. Here lies the crap. For the Grand Old Party, the conservative is forced to vote for the very slim pickings while thinking to themselves "Is there anyone moderate"? So as the Democrat is wondering "how far to the left will my favorite affiliation candidate go as a progressive"? You see, we do have a dilemma on our hands.

Maybe the way to achieve a balance in candidates is in the way we choose the final voting procedure. The election which has only the last remaining few who have gone through the "shaving down" by primaries. None of us have been completely happy with the results of who ends up in the final election. If we pay attention to the rest of the country and the individual states elections, we will know what idiots or saints will be sitting in the Rotund. Don't you get it? I have been blown away by the ignorance which sits in the lawmaking body, voted in by the even more ignorant constituents. Or worse yet, not voted in by the general population, but re-districting of states for voting has disallowed millions of voters in our country. Shame.

So if we consider the initial candidates with more attention paid to the way the politician will act in Congress or The House after the election. Does any of us think that the current people in the legislative branch has any idea what the population wants? More so, do you think they care? Here is where the line must be drawn to show what a candidate can bring to the "big boys/girls table".

Now decide that the only way to live in this country is to exercise your civic duty and help the rest of the people out by voting for logical and sensible laws. Start the movement by looking around at the people in your current lives and how they are able to survive. Given many options, we all must realize that ignoring problems only make them worse. The problems then bleed over into other levels of existence corrupting people, creating desperation, and losing sight of the big picture on our planet.

OK. I have been thinking about how to categorize the schmucks and their agenda versus my own. I can decide that in my personal life the following items have a direct influence upon my living happily and safely.

Women's Rights
Healthcare
Refugees/Immigration
More war or no war?
Minimum wage increase
Human Rights/ food/Shelter
Education/Student loans eliminated
Environment

Militarization of Police in the USA
Alternative Energy development
Utility company rip offs
Poisoning water/soil/pollution/fracking
Rents on homes/Cost of living
Gas prices
Food prices
Water rationing/drought conservation
Fire/police/hospitals/research/CDC
Infrastructure
Social Security Preservation
Medicare increase coverage
Banks being prosecuted/Wall Street crimes
GOP leaders being prosecuted War Crimes
Stop overspending on Bullshit lawsuits
(Benghazi/ACA/ etc.)
Veteran's care/disability/ after care
Child care/ immunizations/schools/food
Animal abuse/criminal neglect
Farming practices/crops/production of food

Now, these are my immediate interests when it comes to the person I think should be in office. The person who is elected to lead the instantaneous needs of the people will be my choice. To quickly correct the terrible things happening to people every day in our country as soon as possible, so we can then advance into the big picture. If the way to survival is to be rebellious and carry "pitchforks", then so be it. If we choose to get off our butts and away from the television set for a moment, perhaps the solutions would be more visible. I think we will all have to comply at some point in our lives with the current amount of pressures we deal with day after day.

If I were informed as to who is participating in the schemes of greedy and corrupt, I might not believe the results. So how can I tell who is "spinning" and who is telling the truth? Of course, this is currently, the exact problem with our voting system. Somehow, the media/social media has taken control of the "facts" and processed them through a "spinning wheel".

If we determine the way the facts have the most influence on our immediate lives, our concerns about things that do not include our "class" should not take precedence. Somehow the average citizen seems to be concerned with the wrong issues. You know what I mean. I see people getting all worked up about foolish things, i.e. Confederate flag waving, Nazi flag waving, gun rights standoffs on illegal grazing lands, fear of the Government "taking over Texas state", Benghazi, E-mails, and Moonshine making. Now, each one of these items has some agenda, as well as has a multiple of people involved in their propaganda machine. Each one of these items has also undergone the "passing of the lie" from media, and social media people.

Every person who watches a television version of the current news is being lied to. Every level of lie begins with the obvious insane remarks to the very subtle messages which are considered subliminal. Each one of these items has been perpetuated by a hate for a person, place, or thing. Every time a person is exposed to another lie, the change of the facts begins a process which allows the lie to be re-created in a fashion needed for a conversation, publication, or broadcast.

We could change the false information by adding so many facts, the people telling the lies would be ultimately confused and unable to perpetuate more lies. Remember, it is easier to recall the truth than a lie. Don't make your own life more difficult by adding the multiple lies which do not concern anyone but those who fall for it.

What I am saying is BACK UP YOUR FACTS. Reveal sources which are unbiased and not with some hidden agenda which will eventually destroy all that you believe. I think the people on this planet all have a common goal. Survival. If we are in the Middle East and the war is raging around us, do we not strive for immediate survival? Can anyone understand that the ease of living in our country is producing some very complacent and lazy people? Now I think we are getting an idea as to how to differentiate our saturation of the lies, but adding facts to the mix.

Chapter 24
Let's go on to the fun part, please?

I am almost certain that everyone in our country is nuts to some degree. I cannot imagine having to go through any of the many changes we have imposed upon our people without having some degree of psychosis. The truth in reality can be a hard thing for some people to grasp. The fear mongering has taken its toll on many people who are just not capable of deciding the better choices in their lives. We compare people by their dollar value, and not their self-worth. We continue to try to cut food from hungry children in school, and allow seniors to die instead of getting care, allowing Veteran's to live on the streets, and continuously destroying our own water sources for sustenance.

We are absolutely insane. Our country has gone so out of whack, we have not allowed anyone to pipe up with any sense of logic. Nobody seems to be professing that we change the archaic system of voting and eliminate the Electoral College. Sheesh folks, the College was imitated because the states couldn't converse with each other in a quick fashion when the ballots were counted, so they had the states represented by the Electoral College to divide and more efficiently count a nation's ballots. Sure, it was good for the year it was created. When you had to wait for telegraph and newspaper result the next day, the process was hard and unable to have instant results like we have now.

Yes, people. I need to reiterate that we have not eliminated one of the things that have held up the voting process for a LONG TIME. Each time the Electoral College is manipulated, the wrong person gets put in office. The population says one thing, and the idiots populating the College say something else. This is not fair. Nobody should have the right to overturn a general populations' voices and words! And yet, we continue to just sit here and let these people walk all over us. At this point, I would hope that some of the readers are getting a little worked up about things that do matter.

We need to be fired up about something in our lives. We cannot just sit around and hope that something might entertain us. How can a caring person go through life without some sort of inner drive that lets us wake up each day and continue on? To be able to be happy and strive for our own "paradise" should be the basis of how we vote for issues, policies, and representation.

I happen to know that the candidates running for most very public offices usually get the most attention. These are also the same candidates who will be brought down through their own demise while they try to run for office. Remember, we have turned the candidates into a reality show with the "surprises" popping out every turn in the race. We have done this. Each and every one of our citizens is making very serious choices based upon the money, glitz, bullshit, and lies we believe. Shame on us. Reminds me of the NFL choices in a football pool based upon the color of their jerseys. Based upon these choices, were the percentage of wins the same as betting based upon the statistics?

Like tossing a coin, the same average statistic will result. The act of a coin toss will not work for knowing what the heck to change in our society. Nor will second-guessing what someone means when they promise to change things on your behalf. How can that be?

How does someone else understand what we are going through unless the candidate is the same class? None of the politicians are normal people. None of these people elected hold the title of scientists, teachers, farmers, or store owners. They are all career politicians. I think that the term limits on these jobs are necessary to increase current ideas, creativity, and forward motion through life. But how do we get this type of agenda to the lawmakers? The same people who are continuously voting themselves raises, and work only a third of the year are creating havoc for the remaining people in the country.

Now for the Dream Team. I have decided that the politicians are all scum. No matter how liberal or helpful they are in the world, most are basically scum. Even the ones who are being so wonderful so as to add the people out in the country as a part of their agenda. They are still scum. They are all narcissists to a certain degree. Each one of these people has a love for their country, but better a love for themselves. Everyone who is drawn to the spotlight has the same characteristic. This is why we have a tendency to fawn over people because of their on-screen persona. We also glorify those who are actors for their roles in certain movies but forget to separate the actor from the acting and understand that they are not the same people.

We are all the same psychological mess. Every person on this planet has some degree of psychosis. Multiple people act out on these brain functions, and others do not. The environment is the reason as well as the surrounding of influences in a person's immediate area. So if we understand that every person we vote for will have a degree of insanity, we can start eliminating the totally insane to moderately nutty characteristic.

We are all sure that the people who we admire are flawless. No? Well, let's add up the virtues versus the flaws. I will ask myself these questions, and many more when I "size up" a political candidate.

- Are they ready to fight for their beliefs or mine?
- Will they be humane and allow refugees or immigrants into our country?
- Will they protect the immigrants who help the economy?
- Will they change their minds on things if the constituents want?
- Do they have a background with common people and have they lived the same way as many in our country?
- Are they an inherited privileged person?

- Are the issues they are defending have anything to do with my lifestyle?
- Have they committed crimes and are under indictment?
- Are they War Hawks?
- Does any of them have an idea as to the racial problem in our country?
- Will they do anything to help the average person to live without oppressing?
- Are they for or against fracking?
- Will they help save our water sources?
- Are they racist, bigoted, or white privileged?
- Have they ever done this job before?
- Do they know how to speak to people?
- Do they practice what they preach?
- Are they taking money from Dirty Sources?
- Have they got any idea what the people want?

I think that I have many other questions which are spawned by this list, and the need to have the added questions answered is great. I cannot choose a Dream Team unless the majority of my needs are met in their ranting and campaigning. I could be wrong, but I am thinking that the people who will open themselves up to public scrutiny will be the better candidates in the long run.

Could there be another way to decide what the candidates are saying? Well, the research part is where the common person will just be lazy and say, aw screw it, I'll just watch the news instead.

Sheesh. I cannot imagine how boring it is to watch a bunch of talking heads lying their asses off and smiling the whole time.

So I continue with the next list and that is the one where I will list the bad and the good stuff.

BAD STUFF

Candidate 1.	Candidate 2.
Loud	Too meek
Obnoxious	Hard time speaking
Too angry	Not passionate enough
Says racists things	
Saying insane things	
Wealthy	
White	
Homophobic	

GOOD STUFF

Candidate 1	Candidate 2
Experienced	Experienced
Some good ideas	Very good ideas
Keeps crowds lively	Excellent voting records
	Better demeanor
	Happy and honest
	Same concepts as mine

If course we will all have our own opinions about how candidates speak to the people. None of us will have the same bad or good listings, and each one will have a different effect on us. And also there will be more than a couple of candidates running for offices. You can see how a normal person would assess each person who would represent them. But here's the rub. The persons who are younger are registering but not voting.

The concept that we have the power and are not using the privilege continues to plague the whole lawmaking process. The people who are making the laws are being placed in the position to command everyone's lives. So why wouldn't we want to make sure that these same people are representing our interests? Sorry, folks. We are completely LAZY.

If we continue to allow the people who certainly do not care about anyone but themselves to ruin our chances of being equal, why would we have fought for equal rights throughout our country's history?

Could this be something that has morphed into the current dilemma of death, terrorism, or fear mongering? Of course it is. The people who will continue to create havoc or frighten with panic-stricken results will also be the same people who will be making the laws for us.

The lists are simple a way to sort out the ways to assist ibn choosing a candidate. The problem remains with the politician in general. We have been instructed that all politicians are corrupt, yet still take pride in putting them into office. We have been complacent to allow others to determine what is good for each one of us. We have stopped caring about how many people are suffering or starving in our own country because we are not looking at it every day. But what about those who are seeing each sad life be taken away?

I do believe that each one of us cares. Most of my friends are completely aware of the damage being done to our environment. All who I speak with have compassion and want animals to thrive and be rescued. Along with most of them, they are not participating in voting or activist activity.

Are we not all activists in some way or another? I have seen many people who will always stick up for the weak when tormented, or rescue people and animals from certain death. I am always proud of my friends who will donate their time and services to assist those who are desperate.

I am also aware of the people who are quick to say "aw, screw them" and not bother to assist or bring aid. Most of the people on our planet are born with compassion. The slow stripping of the humanity throughout our over-privileged population is what has been creating such a corrupt bunch of candidates.

We are required to understand the people we are voting for, yet most of the population does not represent the overall general population of our country. We have no teachers, scientists, agricultural population, environmentalists, or equal rights representation. Think about it. The people who represent us are all lawyers or judges.

Most every person in congress and representatives are nowhere near the common USA citizen type. Not one. There used to be many people of multiple distinctions representing their constituents. We have changed the leaders to include a massive law background so as to manipulate laws and make people confused.

Chapter 25
Now is the time

I think that having some kind of list is ultimately a wise overview of the personal association with the candidate. The actions of their deeds will help to fuel the momentum.
I think that a number of roadblocks we come up against has everything to do with how we do our civic duty. Most of us are not only unable to come up with the time to get to the polling place, but we seem to have transportation problems frequently.

Lots of states have been crippled with voting requirements increases. Also, there are many who have re-districted so crazy people cannot figure out how or where to go vote. I know of people who have now over an hour in travel time to get to a polling place because the districts are so far removed from their homes.

So now I am totally confused. We need to vote, and some people are making it more difficult. What could possibly be the problem here? Each one of our votes matters. Our lives matter, and our resources to make sure we survive as a species. How could someone wake up every morning and want to kill people by poisoning their water, or allowing them to starve to death? Something is truly wrong with this society, and none of us seem to be able to correct the error. We cannot get further forward if we allow greedy and disgusting people to ruin the planet for the rest of us. We cannot possibly survive on this planet if we allow the same people to eliminate every resource we have left. So what can we do?

First of all let's remember some of the past things that liberal voters have brought forth to our lifestyles:

- *The GI Bill*
- *Endangered Species Act*
- *Environmental Laws*
- *The Space Program*
- *The Peace Corps*
- *Americorps*
- *The Civil Rights Movement*
- *Earned Income Tax Credit*
- *Family & Medical Leave Act*
- *Consumer Product Safety Commission*
- *Americans with Disabilities Act*
- *Freedom of Information Act*
- *A Women's right to control their reproductive future*
- *Allowing citizens to view their own credit records*
- *The Internet*
- *Balancing the federal budget*
- *The Brady Bill (5-day wait on handgun purchases for background checks)*
- *Lobbying Disclosure Act*
- *"Motor-Voter" Act*
- *The Voting Rights Act*
- *Unemployment Insurance*
- *Medicare/Medicaid*

- *Food Stamps/WIC*
- *Social Security*
- *Peace between Israel and Egypt*
- *Peace between Israel and Jordan*
- *The Department of Education*
- *The Department of Energy*
- *The Department of Transportation*
- *The Department of Housing and Urban Development*
- *Labor Laws*
- *The Marshall Plan*
- *Winning World War II*
- *Food Safety Laws*
- *Workplace Safety Laws*
- *The Tennessee Valley Project*
- *The Civilian Conservation Corps*
- *The Securities and Exchange Commission*
- *Women's Right to Vote*
- *Universal Public Education*
- *National Weather Service*
- *Product Labeling Laws*
- *Truth in Advertising Laws*
- *Morrill Land Grant Act*
- *Rural Electrification*
- *Public Universities*
- *Bank Deposit Insurance (FDIC)*
- *Centers for Disease Control and Prevention*
- *Public Broadcasting*
- *Supporting the establishment of Israel*
- *The United Nations*
- *NATO*

I would hope that we have basically seen what benefits are available to all of us if we continue to lean forward. We have all of the skills, technology, ideas, innovation, incentive and desire to keep inventing things and making our lives fun and easy. We also know that we didn't just run out one day while these wonderful rights and benefits fell into our laps. We have made the changes by voting and creating ways to help guide our representatives in the House. I have personally voted on the Women's Right to Choose and multiple other rights which people are trying to take away to this day. I voted on this in 1972. And they are still trying to make this law go away.

We keep adding to the way each of the generations will perceive things. The way we look at reality and how things are put into a perspective that generates wonder. I am sure we have the power to do these things, but the root of the barriers remain the same. I feel that the people who want the power also think that power comes with money. I am still so very sorry about how everything in our lives has become a "value system" and no matter who you are, apparently someone has a value on you. We see this in every election where the goal is to raise the most money. Wait, who can raise the most money for what? To pay people to pay other people? To pay for food and lodging? What are the people charging who are being paid? And for what are the charges that would need millions and millions to accommodate the payment? Who's getting the dough?

The way we see this money generating season seems to be a way to make more people rich, adjust the donations to the laws and create the result in who gets elected. OK. So that seems like when rich people go out shopping and if they have more money, they can buy whatever they want. Shopping for a government official has been in practice for centuries. Some are caught and corruptible, and others are getting by just fine. Some officials haven't got a clue of how their official position is run, and will spend a large amount of time dipping into the funds to make their own lives easier. After they have satisfied their own cravings, they will begin to hand out the rewards (leftovers) to the folks who helped get all the money which purchase him /her so well.

See? We have created a certain place in our society where money is more valuable that logic, life, air, water, survival, and coexisting. Money has been the problem all along. We know it. You all know it. We all just stand there and hope we can have more money to survive another day, week, month, or year.

The dang population is dwindling away because of money. People are killing each other/everyone because of money. Everything that has happened to our judicial system, both the laws and the judges/police/lawyers have made it impossible to survive without stealing or being desperate to rob so as to exist another day. If we were able to see that the system was not working, how come none of us even batted an eye when the congress was plotting to create a full on privatized criminal system? From policing all the way to prisons our system has been corrupted, manipulated, sucked dry for funds, skimmed down to exclude job opportunities without some sort of "militarized and privatized" indoctrination.

I would have presumed our legacy as a powerful and wonderful country was capable of lasting forever. I always thought how nice life would be to live in a country where everyone was wishing they could live. I wanted to be a part of the people immigrating and mingling other cultures with that of our own. The events would have been wonderful, and the diverse population would be as interesting and incredible as I dreamed.

To have access to Native culture, and America before industrialization would have been my dreams. I could stand in the middle of a beautiful desert or forest and think of how many generations of humans walked in my path. How many different types of people lived off the land and made the areas as their own. As I hike along the edges of the Oregon Coast beaches, I think of Sacagawea and the Lewis and Clark expedition. I am stunned by the views and always wonder what it must have been like to see the Pacific coastline for the first time. Or even the chance to live there and survive off the land could make my dreams come true as an incentive when a first time Pioneer of the migration Westward.

I could have been better off just imagining the way they were happy and free back then, but I would have been sadly mistaken for feeling as such. The harsh weather and brutal coastline of the northern areas have always been a barrier in the prediction of our ever-changing earth's weather patterns. Yes, the climate is changing and we also know that since we have been taking records, we know the weather has been very changeable. We just screwed up and forced it to progress faster than the resources could be replenished.

Voting for certain issues helps to not only have a say in the outcome but a better understanding of how the laws affect each of us is the bottom line. I think we are aware of this but still don't feel like participating. Of course, we all know why. Corruption. Wall Street and stocks, Banks and Hedge fund people, money and overseas baking, and of course the families which own the banks and have all the money. The sign that everything up for grabs is being vacuumed up and stashed in other places. A bank is a place that will lend you money if you can prove that you don't need it.

This is the mantra we common folks have to abide by. The big corporations are pretty quick to lend for that all mighty interest which turns money into debt. Big banking and Corporations are very quick to enjoy money and flow of money as a power and control factor in a citizen's life. You all know they love to own people, and we are all owned. Not one of us is really free here in the USA or the world for that matter. Whoever holds the debt, is the slave-owner. The working by we slaves is to replenish the debt which we continuously keep getting into. We know why the way we hoped to have Democracy was based upon the voice of the people who are citizens. We are fully capable of handling the civil task of speaking out on a ballot, but yet we are thinking that rebellion is basically just not participating.

If I am concerned about the environment, then I will vote on the issues which affect my locale. I will also take into consideration how the environmental impact will then affect my community. How can people constantly vote against their own interests? How can the serious act of changing lives be thrown away so as to make another wealthy corporation move their funds to another country?

I think the last few paragraphs are simple to answer with the start of the sentence. Corruption. Greed and Sloth are probably in there as well, so the outcome remains the same and the people involved are never the least bit grateful for your donation to their wealth. You see, not participating allows the foolish lambs who cannot possibly decipher their own needs, choose the flock leaders need for more money and profit. Rather the Sheepherder leading his flock off a cliff without any consideration of the flock.

You know we can do this. We all can revolt and show the elected politicians that we are participating. The people who have been spending a century or more trying to eliminate the rights of others are truly amazing. How can a person possibly wake up every day and hope that they can oppress or damage another human's psyche?

There seems to be a problem with the way we have been programmed to care for others. Somewhere along the line we have been directed to a more hateful and intolerant place. I have never seen so much crap online and in the media where everyone knows the basis for most of the insanity in murders, violence, destruction, and death is race. Why are we so geared to think that since we have a different pigment in our skin we are the least bit different? Sheesh.

Pigment is environmental. Period. If you live in certain areas, the sunlight rays will be providing skin tone to accommodate the surrounding geographical areas. That's it. Nothing about the darker your skin the less of a person, as well as the whiter your skin the more of a person? I am the daughter of an Anatomy/Physiology Professor I know there is NO difference in human physiology. We are a species, for cripes sakes. Just as the blonde jokes come forth, and the black jokes spew, with the Italian jokes following, so is the boring reference to color or gender.

Now we know that voting is something that remains sacred to we who have effected changes in the policies and have been lucky enough to have the laws of the land upheld, we move to another dilemma. The striking down of very valuable laws and rights which have helped guide our nation for the past 50 plus years.

We know that the Supreme Court has been infiltrated by foolish and conservative puppets of corporations, but are we aware that the changes are needed to make the laws remain intact? I know many people who have a very hard time understanding how the government process works. I could freely say that 90% or more of my friends and acquaintances have no idea who our Supreme Court members are. I also know they would not be able to name more than maybe one or two. Nobody is able to even give me a moment of simple civics class basics when I ask about sources, or to possibly elaborate on statements. As well as the same phrases come out of their mouths which mimics the television media "spin rooms" which end up in meaningful conversations regarding politics. The sadness also behooves me to want to help explain the proof/facts and help people get in tune with how they need to try to think critically.

Most folks are aware of the things I have mentioned in this book. Sometimes I believe people to be rather intelligent in reasoning. The possibility of the outcome not being what you want is probably the hardest thing to overcome as a voter. To have had to suck it up and be governed by a foolish or uncaring President remains the many years for me of Nixon, Reagan, Ford, Bush, and Bush Jr. We had a very hard time throughout these leaders in office, and we have been plagued with the outcome of bad policy making to this day.

Yet, the fools up on the Hill seem to keep wanting to cut things that are helpful to the country's population, while extending the 80% budget to the military? WHAT IS THIS ALL ABOUT? The stuff these clowns keep complaining about are literally a fraction of a percent in budget, yet they still want to cut our meager funds? This act is where the "Slave owner" gets everything and the people starve and die while making the "Massa" all the profits. Oh yes, a corporatist attitude from the very beginning, and the current level of this greed/corruption is still off the scale.

Perhaps the solution is to just get involved. Each one of us has a rebellious side that is destined to be released in assistance to the rest of us out here. We can help those who have no idea how to do this act of voting. We could start a revolution of people who are just pissed off that "not voting" didn't work. The population is certain to win if we all can group together, no matter what our background, status, color, religion, or gender displays.   Could this be the way to make the process more respectable and less "purchased" by the big corporations? When each person becomes educated about the obvious changes around them, the activity of creating a survivable existence then becomes a community effort.

When we work together the outcome is far greater. The amount of effort put forth by a collective process seems to make everyone happier. I would tend to believe that our process in making voting rebellious, interesting, powerful, and verbal is the secret in being a contributing member of society. If I can help to create a better place for those who have been oppressed or those who are still being pushed around, then I know I have done my best. I have also been able to use the tools around me in voting and the knowledge of the laws a major part of my words when I speak out. So I suppose it's true, I worked myself up from nothing to a state of extreme poverty.

I am sure that each person who has spent their adult lives working at a job can understand how the phrase "work hard and you'll be successful" has been tossed around recently. We have also been directed to understand the wages paid currently are sufficient. Goodness me. Not only is the living wage hideous, but the whole nation is suffering with nowhere to live. There is nothing that spawns illness, destruction, and mental health issues like poverty ignored. When a person works

147

more than one job and still must live with more than 4 roommates to get by, there is certainly something wrong with the total picture.

Chapter 26
When We Learn to Rock the Vote

We have been able to "Rock the Vote" for a long time but seem to forget how cool the act of speaking loudly with actions means to others. I am aware how people are affected when laws are put forth and the benefits of voting for everyone's interest can be so positive. The changes in people's lives can produce incredible citizens and outstanding contributions to our whole country.

The act of not participating takes as much effort as does participating. Think about it. A person who would actively not vote to "teach the system a lesson" are the same people who are the loudest to complain when they are not appeased. I have also noticed that people think they are so cool to not vote when we are all out here doing what we can to legalize weed, keep the right to choose available for all, keep the voting process available and easy for all, as well as rights to marry, adopt, worship, and live however we all wish as a form of coexisting.

So we know how to think a little more about the people who are taking away from our livelihoods and those who are trying to contribute. I think we can proceed in using the vote as the best power tool in the garage. When the best tool for the job is a simple day aside to make a lasting impression on society, then use that thing! Can you imagine how awful it may be to someone who has never been given the opportunity to vote? Can you realize that the people involved with making sure people lose their rights have been voting all along?

Remember, this heinous action of gerrymandering districts, refusing voter ID or stagnating the opportunity to vote has been in effect for a long time. The first sign was the obvious Florida Chad event where the hundreds of thousands of votes were not counted because of a little physical piece of "chad" flashing not able to be read properly. Hmmm, Florida huh? Sounds suspicious to me since Jeb Bush was Governor in 2000 and the election was handed to his brother.

"Then a five-to-four conservative majority on the U.S. Supreme Court in a logically tortured decision ruled that a complete recount in Florida would be a violation of the Fourteenth Amendment's equal protection clause because different States' Counties have different ways of counting the votes. At that point, Gore was behind by only a few hundred or so votes in Florida and was gaining ground with each attempt at a recount. By preventing a complete tally, the justices handed Florida's electoral votes and the presidency to Bush, a stolen election in which the conservative activists on the Supreme Court played a key role.

Even though Bush Jr. lost the nation's popular vote to Gore by over half a million, he won the Electoral College and the presidency itself. Florida was not the only problem. Similar abuses and mistreatment of voters and votes occurred in other parts of the country. A study by computer scientists and social scientists estimated that four to six million votes were left uncounted in the 2000 election.2" *-New York Times, 15 September 2002; the investigators were from California Institute of Technology and Massachusetts Institute of Technology.*

Or perhaps in 2004 when the next Florida incident had to do with the machines failing to register tallied votes, and as well the thousands of actual votes that were "lost" and couldn't be found, or the thousand who were "purged" out of the system. Hmmm. Again, thanks, Jeb, you did your part to screw us from all the way across the continent. Shameful and foolish voting tactics, which we all are now very aware of. "In Florida some 50,000 voters were purged in 2004 (in addition to the many purged in 2000), many of them African-American, who still were unable to vote by 2006. In various states and counties the subterranean war against electoral democracy continues." *-New York Times, 9 November 2006. Michael Parenti: Article; The Stolen Presidential Elections: (updated version, May 2007); http://www.michaelparenti.org/stolenelections.html*

I understand that the electoral process can seem complicated, but this activity indicates more of a thought out process and contrived to create a place for any puppet the powerful and wealthy may have needed. Or perhaps we should ask the pressing question: Why do Americans choose from just two people to run for president and 50 for Miss America? Perhaps Trump can answer that one.

I am also sure that anyone who reads a book, or anything for that matter, will have a better means of processing thought. Sort of a given, but sometimes people are unable to think logically or critically. I am sure that the most of our public schooling has given us the tools to think, but the actual classes which should have been taught to us in high school were that of "secretary, accountant, stenographer, nurse, housewife, mother, and teacher". Nothing else, pretty much we women had no choices in careers but the above mentioned. We had to fight for the glass ceiling to be lifted. We did this.

We are the same people who were living in the era where we could make it count for all of our fellow citizens.   We fought for many things that the Millennials take for granted. Boomers take for granted the past generations of activists who have voted our sacred rights into the law of the land. The changes can come quickly and effectively if we will get together and make our voices known.

What are we waiting around for? I am sure each and every person who can read or wants to party on with the vote can find it within their "busy schedules" to Rock this bitch. The power is in our hands and we must school a few people and show them that they cannot only be rebellious but can be a total non-conformist and still speak out against the bullshit being dumped in our laps. The conservative crap is not working in the new millennium.

We are not really that stupid are we? Come on, I am sure that each person is capable of understanding that the old ways did not work and that is why we proceed forward with new technology to become better. Better in every way. Better people, and better fellow human beings. So now we are aware of the wonderful changes that happen when we participate in voting. And we snicker while the conservative people want everything to be the way it was in the 20's, 30's, or even farther back in time.

I cannot imagine how we could possibly go back in time and think that the ways of the past would be relevant to the current century. I am always surprised at how people will cherry pick the one thing they might have liked about the "old days" and try to thrust it on others a century later. Same with the bullshit about trying to inflict religion into the constitution or the laws which govern a "separated from church and state" country.

People need to stop trying to say that their religion or politics is the only way for others to think or behave. Gosh, I have no time to spend running around for a "Call to Mosque", or make it to a church facility each and every Sunday, only to be a hypocrite and denounce anything shoved down my throat anyway. I am stunned when I hear people tell me that I am not capable of voting or having a political opinion based upon my gender. I am tired of not being taken seriously when I have done the research and the common response in an adversary's ignorance is, "because Fox news told me so..." And the person usually thinks that the response is the "because I said so" answer to stop further comments on the subject.

Man, the possibilities of ruling the world when one can make millions of people who lose all reality, logic, physiology, physics, nature, and species adaptation give them nothing they need to survive in return. What a very strange thing to be "well versed in" for a living. But, none the less, the conservative follower thinks that the old days were wonderful (though it was horrible), women were inferior, white males were/are the only leaders and the free food and welfare doesn't come to them unless the little people vote for the red guy.

A possibility that most of the people fooled by the right wing extremists are these same ones who were standing there at Bundy Ranch ready to kill "them nasty Feds" instead of allowing the laws they voted in to be enforced. They are same people who will picket a gay wedding and make sure you know that you are going to Hell because they said so.

I am more certain of my close friends and their views as I am with the rest of the country. But it seems that the rest of us out here are thinking the same way. I also believe that the masses are not anywhere near as conservative as the very small amount of people in our country who seems to be running things. Are we not mindful of the ways which we are being manipulated? I always say that it is one thing to be taken advantage of and not know it. It is truly another to be fully aware of the taker.

I just know that we are all on the same page here. To have fought for the rights that are being removed one by one remains a hard pill to swallow. Each person who has spent any time checking the statistics and facts regarding certain legislation has been let down. I know that my agenda has been shot to Hell in a moment as I saw the Voter's Rights Act struck down, and one of the Supreme Court member that voted to have it abolished was black! How is this possible? How can people even believe that any person would think controlling the racist's states with bigoted, hateful, gerrymandered, ID locations shut down, and discrimination laws are removed? The concept was (so they say) is that we didn't need them any longer. Racism was over. Holy crap.

That is not even close to being the truth, and we allowed those people in office by not voting? What fools we are. We thought that if we ignored the process, they would just fade away.

So now that we are cognizant of the way these people control each of us, don't you think it's time that we taught them a little lesson about humanity? I would love to show them that we can proceed through life without having to control others. We can find a common ground to intermingle and we could possibly share knowledge about things related to our species. Not just what you have parked in your garage, or the house you own. And could it be possible for us all to make sure the other people are not totally destroyed by poverty for a change? Gosh, if you all haven't noticed the increase in people who are begging on every corner, and who are sleeping in gutters because the rent is so high anywhere.

Haven't we seen the same budget for our country and noticed that the 80% spending has been on the military? Food and shelter are not even a 0.0002% amount of overall funding to keep people from dying. And the same people who are in need of nutrition assistance, are the ones who are voting for the people taking away the programs. Then, they "blame Obama".

Can't we see that the GOP integrated system has begun to unravel? The age of information has begun to provide multiple people with the facts. The media is not the only source to check on things relevant to voting. This option in research is the drive that makes me feel like I am winning in every vote. I am able to see the fraud, and vote it the heck out of there. I am able to be one with many thousands (if not millions) of those who want to believe that my vote matters. And it matters in a huge way to other people fighting for the same rights.

I am also very quick to reprimand those who would want to have the system the way it was in the past. How could the wheel become something other than what it is? How could a person think that we would have to go back and re-invent something that evolves?

You see, the aspect of knowing everything changes in life is the secret to having a political opinion. We all are conscious of the way other people can be sucked into the void of lies and deception. I have seen the action take place in front of my eyes. While a person is watching an event, another is telling them that does not relate whatsoever to what they think and that what they are viewing is something else. They can actually make people see something different. I think magicians do this in their shows, and the skill seems to be passed around from one bullshitter to another in different levels.

Every person that stands up on that soap box is either just trying to get attention or trying to make you believe something which is relevant to your life. Each one who is selling their "wares" will tell you anything you want to hear so as to receive your attention. Once attention has been achieved, the crap comes out and the mesmerized victim has been drawn in.

The way that a politician has an effect on a person is usually through their wallet. The act of coercion is a very good method to sway someone to believe they will be able to make them rich. Or perhaps the politician will make sure that the potential voter will prosper if they vote the way the politician wants. How can we be sure that they have any credibility to their speeches? How could we possibly know which politician is telling the truth or has any means to make our lives better? None of them are telling the complete truth. Just remember that NONE of them have only you or your family in mind. Not one. Not Bernie or Hillary… you are not the ONLY thought on these people's minds.

If we can just get to the fact that the leaders see us as constituents and not family members. They do, however, make it possible for us to make changes in the way we are governed. Some elected officials so, but most forget who got them to the elected office in the first place. I also am very distressed about the fact that the elected official is more apt to ignore the people's needs and start playing around in the national scene by voting in or out serious laws.

I have noticed that none of my friends even have any idea how the elected officials in other states and are the very same ones passing insane laws which affect me! How can my friends in other states send a total fool to the House and think that they will not wreck everything in sight? Especially the freshmen freaks on the GOP side. Man, those people are so into screwing people because they can sit far away and hide while they squash every little bug in their way to being the "world leader". The quest for power is so obvious, I am embarrassed about the things these people say.

The political people on the conservative levels are professing women should enjoy being raped and have babies instead of an abortion, domestic beatings are fine, the Bible should be the only book read, a government needs to be dominated by religion, children work in factories, or that women should not even be voting. So what I am seeing is the past where the year could be anything from 0-1960. How did we possibly get fooled to believe that these days were better for anyone but white males? I cannot even begin to explain how I was raised to believe that women had only a few places on the earth, and none of it included major achievement possibilities in politics, leadership, military, corporations, professorial honors, owners, and self-made millionaires. We were sure that when we voted in the early 70's there would be a major change in the way the world would turn out because peace and love were the driving forces.

Well sure it was our directive back then to have the most liberal and artistic elements involved in our decision making. We would allow the debate in any forum to see how the laws could affect us. During the 1972 election, our plans were to make sure the ERA was on the floor and would be the law of the land in our constitution (where it still sits today without it being enacted). We got to vote for the Right to Choose laws which became the law of the land, and the same law that the minority conservatives are still trying to thwart. The laws that have held up over the years still have enemies. The people who would be the first to tell you what to do are the same people who want you to be eliminated from any process where they will not achieve power or wealth.

They do not care about you. "They" are the conservatives and their religious agenda and "you" are the people who are free to not accept this way of living by people who don't even care to know you. We are the people who will change things to include all people and not just a chosen few who have money, and would be happy to remove yours at any time to make their wallet fatter.

If you think about how many people will have to learn to deal with the way the laws are enacted, then perhaps the way to have elections matter is to vote. We are all sure that the loudest bitching about the current laws are made by those who didn't bother to vote, or if they did the information did not reveal the true meaning of their vote. This is a possibility which stems back to the part of this book where I indicate the equivalent of voting information pamphlets top that of a driving test. None of the questions make sense, and the answers seem to be the opposite of the question. Yes means no and no means yes. This is a confusion which makes the art of voting intelligently an impossibility at times. Someone needs to make the issues more conceivable by those who have had to go through the USA school system. Which basically means, the level of intelligence is not up to the issues and laws being voted in.

If the law says that the fella next door to me can dig up my back yard because he has mineral rights, I am angry. If the law says that I cannot be angry because the guy is digging up my backyard then there is something wrong with the law in the first place. Most laws are based on logic. I say most laws because there are still some very foolish and ridiculous laws on the books that need to be weeded out and changed to accommodate the current year. There are still laws that say you cannot have a duck on the east side of the street and you can't have a chicken on the west side in some states. Some laws were enacted in the 1800's and earlier, and remain on the books without weeding out the absolutely crazy laws.

Chapter 27
Now, who can I piss off first?

To be able to vote with a sense of rebellion starts with the adversaries who would be very happy to destroy anything that stands in their path to wealth and power. If you are a radical from the 60's you will remember who we were fighting against, and what the theme was for our rebellion. From the Viet Nam war to Rock and Roll, we fought for our freedom to express ourselves without being thrown into a prison. Did we make headway? A little. Most were thrown into jail, or arrested in protest marches. Most were beaten and battered by police and military. A lot of people were killed and lives destroyed by the nature of the protests and the severity of the oppression.

We all had something that made our blood boil and the need to change the ways was being manipulated. The times are not different now. The only problem is that the people who were fighting the fight are older and not interested in how the planet is dwindling and the resources are becoming scarce. It appears that most of my generation is so wrapped up in excessive debt or lack of income they are unable to figure out what to do next. So the only way to be able to get by is to complain about the situation, the government, and the lack of jobs. Instead of trying to find another way to make a living, or trying something different for work, we seem to just become complacent and allow this to be the norm.

Working for anyone is not fun, but if one can find a job that inspires, intrigues, or excites a person the long haul will be wonderful. I know that my skills and interests have been a super way to make money in the arts or music field, which has always made me happy.

Doesn't this dilemma in our current world make you all a little squeamish? You all should know religious wars and killing in the name of an invisible dude in the sky makes me crazy. As much as I can be as aloof as the remainder of the population in our country, I will also spend more time figuring out the facts, unlike the lazy folks.

We are all aware of the massive problem with people's education. We are also now more aware of how people have been "dumbing us down" so as to strike fear. Now, since we are knowledgeable about this act, why are we so complacent? Now is the time to create a safe place for the rest of us to avoid the people standing up and shouting that we are all doomed. The folks that are quick to judge, crucify, and destroy anything different than their beliefs are the same people who brought you war over and over. They are the same people who love to confuse and dodge anything constant. So, now who can I piss off first?

I presume it will be the folks that wants all people of color exported from our country, although the color of this country was already multiple and beautiful before the white folks came in and killed everyone. The lovely "founding fathers" who decided that the Natives were not allowed on their own lands while proceeding to murder and destroy them was normal back then. To establish a country based upon murder and theft still sticks in my craw. BUT we are a land of immigrants. Oh wait, the same people who make up this land are being told to leave because they are a different color? Or maybe because we were already greedy and corrupt when we arrived here on this continent and just "wanted more" as usual.

Perhaps my anger is with the Crusades who murdered and tortured millions of people all in the name of their invisible dude in the sky. The perpetual bickering about which invisible dude in the sky is better than the other people's dude in the sky. Doesn't this sound totally asinine?

I read a meme which showed two girls reading each other's "Bible/Quran" and each of them said their book says to kill the others who don't use their book. And everything that the other's book stated was to destroy and kill the other people's beliefs. So, what they were saying was that each of the girls was laughing because their respective "books" were telling them to hate, kill, destroy, and fear the others. The rules of each book were so foolish and made no logical sense that the younger people were finding it funny. Bad news. People are basing their entire lives on the killing, raping, destroying and eliminating everything that is western or current in the millennium.

OK, so now get this… these people will die for these insane and unusable biblical "rules" which have nothing to do with the 21st century.

Remember, these documents were supposedly written thousands of years ago, and just look how nice the Religious bullshit has turned out for the people who choose to have religion as their country's basis. Their land is destroyed, ruined, and resources stripped. All in the name of the invisible dude in the sky who apparently isn't the same invisible dude as the folks they are fighting. This is why we choose separation of Church and State because the religious crap gets in the way of common sense.

Oh, and perhaps we can look a little deeper into why the Churches pay no taxes, but are in desperate need to control our way of life and our country. Please explain to me how I can take advice in current times from a complete figment of some people's imagination? Of course, we think that the churches are foolish for putting in their HUGE two cents for EVERY law that is up to be passed in our country. How is it possible to have a whole democratic system based upon religion? Rather a contradiction in terms. Again, that invisible dude in the sky is going to make the laws? Where did our logic go? How are we so foolish as to truly think that by doing nothing but praying, something will be accomplished? Sounds pretty lazy to me. Sitting there with your hands folded while the rest of us are out here healing, caring for the sick, helping the folks on the streets, fighting the murderers, and trying to clean up our planet.

Sheesh, folks if you see a drowning person, praying will not save them at that moment, in that time. ALSO, the concept that everything happens for a reason is total bullshit. We perpetuate change. ALL people can make a different outcome from a common formula. There are always exceptions to the "rules'. Tax the churches, and maybe we can be a little more equal adding to the governing of our country.

As well the NFL and big time sports need to get their sorry asses out of politics. Each endorsement, every billion goes into the usual wealthy hands. The NFL (and other sports NBA, etc.) were supposed to contribute heavily to the local areas so as to keep the city sponsoring a team and arena a profitable program. Once again, after the minimal contribution to the cities, the sports folks are raking in billions, and not spreading it around. Instead, they are lobbying for GOP and the usual suspects to keep them non-taxable, and retain their status so as to make billions more.

Of course, we realize that all the sponsors and contributors to the sports programs are the same who are making out like bandits in revenues. They are also the same people who are running negative ads on TV, joining in with low wage workers and adding to the descending income for all the normal folks. If we are aware of the same people who profess a wholesome and good environment for all, and catch them with mistresses and poking little boys.

We also know that for some reason, the "conservative" person in the country seems to disregard this horrible activity, and still elect the same people. Remember, these are also the same people who are in the clergy and have been caught and exposed for child predatory acts. And we just say, oh well… Brother looks like the continuous hypocrisy stands out so tall and prominent in our logical minds. Yet, the same people "dumbed down" are just like little sheep following their shepherd.

We also can piss off people who have no idea how the arts and liberal music dominate human nature. The same people who would burn your rock and roll records and denounce the Beatles in the 60's are the same unwise people who cannot even remember that this occurred. These people are the same ones who insist that rock music is evil and the devils game. How is this possible?

How can a combination of sound notation be evil? How can the people who hate rock, musicians, instruments, events with music, or instruction of music even exist? How does a person eliminate the sweet sound of a bird singing? Oh man, this complete ignorance gets my goat. I can understand how certain music may be irritating to some, but the appreciation should be there, at least. But to eliminate music and styles by banning or burning the items? Makes no logical sense, and most people cannot even fathom how music could not be a part of a living creature's life. To make music for a living seems to piss people off sometimes.

I have seen many who think I should be working in a factory (clocking in on a time card) and being miserable like the rest of the world. I think not. I will just continue to piss off those who have wrinkles and frown lines from spending their whole life doing things they hate. Me? Well, I don't look my age because I spent my adult life playing music for a living, and apparently that pisses some people off. Good, then my work here is done!

Voting pisses people off too. The most conservative nut case is sure that the radical activist will not bother with the system of voting. As a matter of fact, they bank on it. The best way to piss off conservatives is to be political and vote. They hate it. They have spent 50 years+ trying to make voting impossible for many. The funniest thing is that they seem to think that we are not aware of their shenanigans,

Not only do they bank on the general public not caring or being lazy, they bank on the information that is spread through the media. Apparently the conservatives would prefer if the constant consumers of propaganda come out to vote, and the remainder "protests" the voting process. They love that! This act is the same as the divide and conquers tactics which usually ends up with educated voters not voting in protest. So irrational and unwise we are. They are happy to see you protest voting. This way they can get their foolish and sheep-like people out to vote for anything they say.

You see, we are aware of this. All of us are aware that the voting is the secret. The one thing that pisses off conservatives is an educated voter. Here is where we have the upper hand. The basic anti-liberal person has an agenda. The thing that they hate the most is when the agenda has been separated by votes. You perceive the divide and conquer thing works the other way around too.

The act of voting has always been a precious and most valuable commodity. Some of us get it. Others keep telling their friends and family that the voting process is "rigged' and we have no say anyway, so why to try to vote If we were to watch the movie "Zeitgeist" we would better understand that voting is truly a way to appease the masses so that they can be controlled. We know this. It is our job to change the voice from passive to aggressive. The masses have risen up in the past and succeeded. If we are so helpless to the wealthy and powerful, they have the advantage. So we can see this voting process as something powerful or ignore the voice we have fought so hard to achieve. Which will it be?

Will we be able to piss off enough people to get them interested in being heard? Or perhaps we will have made enough noise to be heard by those who are not participating. I am hoping for the latter because the oppression and being cast aside is getting on my nerves. I want to make people so angry that they will have no choice but do something about it. They will have to participate because the only way to achieve health, air, water, and sustainable resources are to make sure the greedy cannot stick their fingers in the pie. We must be strong and acknowledge that some people will not participate not to matter what is going on around them. We cannot change them, and please do not attempt to do so. Trying to change people makes very little sense. Why would a person spend valuable time trying to change people's minds about political, racial, religious and moral issues? Makes no sense to me.

I hardly believe that intense conservatives would have any idea about reality, current surroundings, and the 21st century. None of them can relate to the present panic and fear mongering with wars breaking out everywhere on the planet. Making people angry is not necessary when being forthright and stable in your message. The only problem is that the same people who would mock your views are the people voting. Now, for what purpose is the anger directed? Thinking about the reasons why people are hateful, angry, frantic, and perpetuated by fear helps me to understand that maybe we are in the midst of a mental health problem gone out of control.

If the ways to piss people off become violent or destructive, then your message is wrong. If you make people angry when telling them the truth, perhaps another method of delivering information to them is necessary. Sometimes the message can be swallowed easily when delivered with respect for another's view.

Here are some ideas to help you avoid confrontational and very angry political discussions. Remember: Sparring with someone who only has one or two vague sources will be very dangerous. Especially if they are violent in their comments. Hopefully some if these ideas will assist to get your message across to a conservative without making them upset or too defensive:

169

- Always be sure that you have their views first. The discussions are easier when you see the degree of fanatics or ideology in their thoughts.

- Remember to keep your statistics to a minimum. Most people who are anti-liberal or just anti-human will deny any statistic, even the law of gravity.

- If you must make a point totally against their conservative ways, the way to appease their common sense is to apply the point to a situation involving the conservative with the empathy directed toward them.

- If you feel the least bit angry about what the people say, remember how much they love to feed revolt. The less you are defensive, the easier it is to get out of there without being punched.

- I try to keep up on the latest redirect and will always know where the sources are for the ignorant rantings. Sometimes when presented with alternative sources without mocking theirs helps them to feel less defensive or aggressive.

- If you choose to recite biblical verses, please remember for every religious "comment" is also another in the same book which contradicts the same verse A good idea would be to learn the same verses in their total context instead of cherry picking the ones you like.

- Once a very angry person is on a rant, the only thing to do is to let them finish. They will say awful and hateful things about humans and animals and it will make you very annoyed. If the person becomes violent and threatens to assault you, get out of there quickly. If you see a weapon on the person, do not even engage them in any conversation regarding politics, religion, or racism.

- When approaching a group of polling persons in the voting areas who are attempting to decline your voter's rights, do not make any scene. You may go elsewhere to file a complaint and will be allowed to vote elsewhere. Do not even attempt to make logical conversation with these people regarding your rights. They will not understand and will fight to the death to deny you a vote.

- If discussing certain Presidential candidates or anything with elections involved with angry people remember to stay restricted in the individual naming. The less you elaborate on the candidates policies to these people the better. They will always say something detrimental to your opinion, and your changing their mind is impossible.

- If you are discussing world politics with people make sure they have some Political Science background. Otherwise, anything outside of their backyard will be impossible to understand. Most people do not even know where Syria is, yet alone the capital of California. If anyone can point out on a map where any country involved in the wars is located, then we can have a discussion, otherwise I will never bother.

- Human rights are never a good topic to discuss with conservative, anti-color, anti-female, and anti-voting rights people. No matter what is said about the need to co-exist, these people are dead against it. Racism is alive in the USA like hotcakes!

- Try not to roll your eyes when they are speaking. This action makes them even angrier and they will call you on the act. They will also divert any foolish comments to another subject, if caught in lies, so just be prepared to hear a lot of skipping around the subject matter.

- If you choose to recite sources, remember for every correct fact logged in the books, the uneducated will choose to recite Bible verses, or just say they saw the same story the other way around. Even though there is oxygen to breathe, they will deny it.

- Shaking of the head indicates domination when listening to these people. They will take this act as a threat and will probably become very angry. They do not like to be considered beneath anyone, even though they are.

- If the obvious extremist has gone so far as to threaten you or your friends with you, enabling them with defensive information will only create a very unsafe surrounding for those who are listening. Just walk away, or leave the public place where they can still visually see you.

- Try to be non-confrontational with any stupid, foolish, or insane comments. The racist comments, gender, lifestyle, religion or politics will fly out of their mouths. The same information will always be spouted and no change is possible to contradict their idea of facts or sources. They will call you names, and the names will be awful.

With any discussion comes information that may or may not be correct. It seems to me that the information that seems the most ridiculous is the basis for some people's arguments. If you have been caught shaking your head or rolling your eyes, the harassment and names like "libtard, fat bitch, or just stupid" will begin to fly. The insinuation that perhaps the Devil is speaking through you, or even the concept that you are a terrorist planted so as to destroy the USA "dream".

How do you possibly have any concept of the way our political system works if the facts you need are so skewed? The possibility that each person so far extreme in their thoughts could be right begins to wear on your better sense of logic and eventually you will have to retreat and try never to indulge or enable the evil conversations which creates such hostility. If the person who provides the heaviest burden on the conversation begins to become physical, the only option is to walk away and stop communicating with them. For the sake of safety, or just to know that in our world people are so angry and always looking for someone to spar with.

Chapter 28
Let's turn this thing into a party!

I know that the solemn act of voting and the massive information that accompanies the process can seem daunting. I have learned to create a different atmosphere in the voting preliminary research area.

I have the idea that is making a Voter Information Party with as much food, drink, and music as possible. You may think that a bunch of people getting blasted and stuffing their faces could care less about the political scene, but if the intention is to hang out and enjoy the people you love, share ideas, and help others to understand the issues, the whole event could be quite cool.

Some people will think that everyone will get wasted and to be able to function when discussing the political sides to every candidate or issue up for a vote. The majority of voters do this every day, and as well they are sitting at home with their cocktail or joint reading the information pamphlets as it is.

I have done this before with many of my friends, and usually we would choose a restaurant, bring out sample ballots and information crap, order dinner, and start running down the list. I have been swayed by other people's input and have mistaken certain issues with an incorrect choice. With the aid of my friends and fellow voters, I have been able to read the ballot with time to spare for dessert and a cup of after dinner coffee. I think I will create more of a party scene this election year, and, of course, invite any friends who would be interested in checking out the new way of learning about the political changes.

Can we turn this into a party? We have partied for candidates, rallies and many other political gatherings, so why not have a party to help people vote? How many people can we help? If we were to allow anyone to come, even the best-informed voters could share their views while possibly learning things simultaneously.

What a blast. Having a bunch of people reading and discussing our future with fun, food, drink and music as a background. We all party for the most foolish reasons, so why not make a serious avoidance something to look forward to in the future? I am one who would always love to show up and see what the rest of my friends or new friends would think about many issues and candidates. We could have music and enjoy more conversation than just politics while still understanding how to make our choices count.

The ways to bring out a better group of voters is to make sure each person has a good grasp on the issues and who is presenting them. We can all be more conscious about those who would try to sway our votes by baffling us with bullshit. Some fall for the foolish rants and silly ideas, but most of us are not falling for it. I have been successful in teaching many people about why we vote. The only problem is I have been trying to teach people how to vote. Since we were not lucky in school and had no way of searching the internet for these solutions, we ended up having to stumble through the process.

While teaching my friends about voting and why we have to donate our time to help others and ourselves, I have learned a few things. I learned that people who vote in all elections did not always understand what they are doing with that power. I have discovered that most people talk a load of political shit and do not even vote. I have also learned that voting for the wrong people or issues can affect more people than just me. I have also discovered the ways to have a fulfilling conversation with other people about sensitive issues without becoming angry or defensive.

Maybe we all could try to give voting another chance. If we have had many reasons for not voting, we should have just as many for the process. Somehow we have to be able to give the voting process a chance to work the way we had intended initially. Democracy is not an easy task. And along with that daunting task comes the responsibility of making choices, creating new methods and laws, while having a say in how we govern as a democratic body.

We had chosen this act over Monarchy and if the choice were to allow the citizens to vote for laws and politicians, then perhaps the process itself should be more exciting. Think of how exciting it would have been like the first female to vote when women finally won the vote. Imagine the first black person to cast a ballot, and how thrilled they must have been to do so. If you could remember the first time you were old enough to vote, give blood, or fight for our country, you would have remembered with a very big grin on your face.

I was an activist before I was 18 years old. My fight was for the 18-year-olds in our country to have the right to vote began when I was 16 in 1970 We were being sent off to war in Viet Nam, but could not vote until age 21. The voting issue was serious because the majority of we who shipped out to war would not have voted in the folks who got us stuck over there. My fight was also for women's right to choose with the Roe v Wade issue in my lap for my first vote. We were continuously marching for equal rights with the ERA in the forefront, and the civil rights fight was right in front. We fought for the right to vote at age 18, and I have never faltered in my obligation. Yes, my glad duty that places me higher on the happy list for achieving goals.

I am hoping that we can all get together and make this one heck of a voting party. I want to start a new trend and make voting a sporting fun time. I want people to look forward to elections and have the information correctly absorbed before going in the booth. We could rock this voting thing, and make one heck of a progressive movement with the voter's parties.

I suppose I have never needed a reason to party, but this one could be the most interesting type of party yet. We could have sample ballots and information so as to help people mark their ballots before they walk into the polling place. Confidence is the key to getting in and out of the voting booth and having a pre-marked ballot allows a no-effort quick vote. This way, your time is not monopolized, and the millions of things you needed to do can be completed without interference.

Don't think for a moment that the process may seem boring and has nothing to do with your immediate world. This process can be the most powerful thing you will ever participate in and the best feeling afterward. To win an election in the laws and measures that I voted on is exciting for me. I had been disappointed before with candidate losses and issues I wished would have passed, but the excitement of participating still rocks my world.

I cannot imagine life without a choice. I understand that as children, our choices were made by our parents, and the outcome was theirs. I also remember the choices for women were not allowed to be made for themselves, so the need for women to continue to vote is essential. The necessity to recruit young people is also high on my list. I am so frightened that the complacency of voters will lead our democratic method somewhere else.

Where could this lack of voting interest lead us? Would the good people stop voting too, and continue to hide the rest of their lives? Will they just give up, have a king/emperor/or whatever to run the country? Didn't we want to escape from England and the Monarchy in the 1600's? Somehow people forget that we founded our country on democracy. We wanted to be able to live our lives without the influence of religion, monarchy, taxation, unjust laws, and enslavement with poverty. The large cities in Europe were having many problems and people were so happy to immigrate westward to escape.

I am certain that the younger folks are not even getting this information correctly in school because they have screwed the history so badly, most of us are still scratching our heads as we discover more information about our country. Our needs are now in the millennium, and the ways have changed so dramatically, the methods must change too.

We have got to start having a good time and being excited about our voting. If we turn this into a party and a totally good time, the voting party could catch hold! Let's rock this vote people. We can make the most of what time we have before they deplete the finite resources. We can change the laws to enhance the environment and stop the fracking boom. We could all band together and throw a CITY vote party, or RAVE the vote with some cool food, music, and a party atmosphere.

Making the voting procedure a whole different look and feel with fun, music and good company would make the process tolerable for all of us. One of us has the same feelings about voting. Most of the weird procedures are the part that makes people shy away. Also, the scrutiny of the polling people who provokes feelings of "Big Brother is watching you" when approaching the voting place. I can understand how hard the process feels, but the need to express your opinions and put in your two cents is why we call our nation a democracy. We are all not taught enough about the way voting is changing people's lives daily. We haven't devised an educational course on how much the process means to our families and the locale in which we live.

None of us have been brought to a polling place and watched the people proceed to vote when in school as a civics field trip. We do not have enough education being taught which shows kids why and how the USA does this act. I do believe that if I had been taught more about the process of voting when younger, I would not have been so frightened the first time I voted. And I still hate the atmosphere of a polling place. The people are quiet like in a library, and the feeling is very somber. No wonder people don't like going to vote.

I remember my parents voted absentee for the last 20 or so years because they were in their winter home during election days. I would have enjoyed the process of marking my ballot and mailing it in so as to not have to see all the poll workers scowling at me when I walk in to vote. I was thinking about how wonderful the voting process would be if we could choose our voting locations and who runs the precincts. I would also like to be the host of a voting party where your friends are there, and the atmosphere is calming. I do think this trend could be so much fun as well as informative! The food and beverages would flow, and the people would want to stay and watch election returns after the polling places close.

The party would continue until the winners were announced and win or lose; the feelings would be wonderful!

Chapter 29
Are you in or out?

Will you be one of the people who will come along with the latest most informed voters? Since we are the ones who are trying to change the foolish laws, and the ridiculous bullshit laws coming from the conservatives. We are not the only ones who think this way. We could take this voting party to the rest of the nation and create a landslide election for forward movement. Can we all just learn how to coexist?

If we took all the non-voters and their excuses and stacked them against the voters who are voting for dangerous people voting against their interests, we would lose everything. We have registered voters, but they seem to ignore the local voting and the state levels which get us all into trouble. The lack of participation is why we are drowning in bad laws and lack of funds. All the money we pay in taxes goes to the corporations who have their hands out, and not to the infrastructure. The money continues to go to the military while spending billions on nothing but new war toys.

We have done this to ourselves, people. We allowed the ignorant and foolish to have carte blanche to our cash, and we just stand here looking like we lost our teddy bear. If we hurry, we might be able to save some things and will have to let go of others. Remembering that we have allowed the bad people to spawn Supreme Court Justices that will continue to eliminate each right one by one. They have already eliminated the Voter's Rights Act and are coming for women's right to choose. They have been at that law for 50 years. As well they will continue to spend money in repealing the Affordable Care Act until they all just die.

I am sure that we can all understand that the voting process is what has brought forth the horrible problems we face today. Police are killing citizens, mass shootings are the norm for our country, and children are dying from malnutrition and poverty. We have the power to change these atrocious problems. We have had the power all along. We seem to be just plain lazy. Most of us are just giving p and not participating anymore. Some, my age, have just stuck to one party, and no matter how stupid, foolish, ignorant, or farfetched the party professes their ideas, they still keep voting the same.

If we could have enlightened a few regular voters to look carefully at the crap so as to weed it out from the correct and good laws, there could have been a different result in Presidents. If we had made the voting party a new trend sooner, perhaps the rest of the right wing folks might have been interested to do the same. Maybe if they all sat around and listened to different views, their choices would not be so insane. Nor would their candidates spew crazy, ideologist fantasy and hope the foolish would believe them. The informed voter is the most powerful person in our country. Empowered with the truth, along with knowledge and facts can create a comfortable voting environment in which to speak your mind.

I know that the whole voting deal seems to be so silly and uneventful, but some of us thrive on the thrill of the run. I think that the political climate has changed to include many people who have never really participated in voting for rebellion.

To rebel against the old ways is a fine start when beginning to create a buzz in politics. Change the laws that pertain to the 50's and farther back in time. Make new laws to include the new problems, or discoveries so as to keep people safe. Creating a foundation for your pathway to the control of the life around you is the goal. Being able to speak out and succeed in changing the bad things about our lives and adding new technology or methods to the way we live should be a fantastic feeling.

Accomplishing the task of voting with confidence is not as complicated as one would think. One does not have to know every statistic, fact, name, year, country, or other detailed information to come to a conclusion. The possibility of weeding out the crap and finding the simple truth remains the goal of a powerful and confident voter. All a person needs to do is rock that deal. If you don't like the bull pucky they sling at you, vote against it! Rebellious voting is also sensible because it challenges the norm. I, myself enjoy being a nonconformist. None of us want to be wrapped up in the same old foolish and ancient rules when we are living in the millennium. Sheesh people, get a clue, this is not the 50's where women are subservient and slavery is not dead. We have passed the same corner every time another election comes up. The same people keep voting for the same 30-year career politicians and the laws get more complicated.

I have been rebellious in my voting habits so as to piss off the anti-human rednecks and succeed in receiving the correct laws and measures for the rest of us out here in the real world. I have also been very happy to have seen the multiple laws change throughout my 43 years of voting. I have seen exciting and groundbreaking changes that I cannot believe I was involved in with my vote. I have been lucky to have voted in a few Presidents, but always happy when my senator gets elected, as well as my representative.

I want to rebel against the boring method of voting, the complicated information packets, and the seemingly wasteful time spent being quashed by the larger turnout for the dim-wits. As we know, the voters in our country have been slowly disenfranchised while we all just sit here with our thumbs up our asses and do nothing. What the heck are we doing while allowing the idiots to control the rules of the game here?

If any of my readers got something from this book it should be that the voting process is not fun, is very boring, and doesn't seem to do much good unless the voters arrive at the polls in droves. We are the reason our country functions. Human resources run this country, and though we have been slowly shoved in a dark corner to feel sorry for ourselves, we had better learn who is running the place. And the power is not with any of the citizens as the process for democracy was intended.

Remember how this country is supposed to run, and how the process has been shaved down to accommodate only the very wealthy. The power has then been diverted to the amount of money a person has. So if the candidates get more money in donations that the next fella, they will win. Apparently, we have arrived at the "pay to win" game, and he who has the most money gets to lead the country! Whoo Hoo! Boy, doesn't that just entice a person to run for political office? Perhaps the aspect of being wealthy, white, and male would be the reason the current shareholders of human bondage are running the Congress and House.

Maybe the only way to receive ownership of our country again is to make our voices heard. Sounding off on the social media does a little but mostly the communication of face to face human contact does the trick. I mean, how many people have you heard recently speak about or complain about the way our current President governs our country? I am sure than in the course of one day; someone will have mentioned the crap going on in our country and the world.

How do you respond? Are you sad and shake your head in dismay? Do you pipe up and say things that might help others in a positive fashion? Or are you the one who will be another grim reaper and profess that we will all be dead soon?

`Questions must be asked about yourself when you begin to feel that the whole country has gone raving mad, and the things that people are saying are so hateful. The white KKK people are trying to kill people of color, and the police are perpetuating the racism by adding more violence and self-motivated reactions instead of calm reasoning.   Everyone is just genuinely angry.

It is my opinion that the dwindling resources are at the root of the frustration humans are having. The cost of water, food, living spaces and medical help is so high that people are ready to rob, murder, and take anything that keeps them alive. We remain poor and the wage gap so large, all of us on this side of the fence are suffering. I do not blame those who are stealing because all of them have nothing, and the uber-wealthy have everything.

So now we all must admit that we all want to be rich and lay around eating bonbons all day. But what is the purpose of working to achieve wealth and just laying around like a beached whale? How can that be the least bit fulfilling? I have noticed that wealthy people who do nothing to assist the world because of their capability in financial stability seem to be hated, sad, and suicidal. We all shake our heads when we hear of a rich person who has killed themselves, or has become a recluse. "How could they have been sad, they had millions of dollars"?

Now we finally understand that having money does not make you happy. More than likely, the excess in your life having millions can cause large problems that will never cease. Some people seem to be Ok with the distribution of their wealth and have been spending millions on assistance to families or communities. Then there are the rest of the greedy money grubbing folks who will just send the money to another country to hide and not pay taxes. These people are the hoarders and will not move the money through our country to generate revenues in other areas.

We are the only contributors to the economy. The middle class and poor are the ones who spend the money in our country, not the wealthy. They spend their money in Europe, or travelling and staying in other countries. The money does not flow in our country, and they will do anything not to be taxed on this dough, so they stash it elsewhere.

The reason I mention this information is because the voters have allowed this to happen. We are in store for a very long ride by those who would be voting against our interests. No taxes for large corporations, safe havens for money stashing, money laundering, sending jobs to other countries so as to make more profits with slave labor, vile and toxic products imported from China and other places. We allowed this to happen. Because; we DIDN'T vote. We watched the States' officials gerrymander and hide these laws inside of other bills that passed.

I think they are only hoping someone doesn't find out how many hidden laws were in the last set of bills that passed? The citizens are finally getting this information, and the people who are secretly stashing little tax loopholes, and sideways laws in bills that have nothing to do with the basic bill contents. Sheesh, we are finding out many things slipped into the passing of laws and bills that had no bearing on the initial bill. I am astounded that the discovery of the additions has only been recent. We have no idea how many years these people have been manipulating the laws and stealing everything we all work hard to achieve monetarily by sneaking in laws sandwiched between other laws.

If just a few of us had paid attention to these bills as they were voted in, we might have been able to call them on the dirty deeds. But since many of us do not vote, how could we have known? What a crappy way to find out that you will be paying a far greater percentage in taxes because you didn't show up at the polls and contradict the wealthy, greedy vote with your own.

You see, WE are the reason the shitty things are happening in our economy. We allowed Bush to get into office; we were neglectful in not voting for the mid-terms so that the laws would not seem crazy like they are now. And mostly, I remind you all that the "fool" we put into office in 2000 was the Supreme Court addition of 2 Justices, unnecessary war with another country, and the raping of our surplus that Clinton built for our country's infrastructure. We also allowed Cheney to move his company Halliburton into receivership of millions in revenues with war by not protesting the bills that included how contractors receive contracts for government jobs. Including the amounts of money these people made by overcharging, building unused structures, and squandering money on luxuries while in the Middle East. What a racket!

As I cried my eyes out when Bush stole the first election in 2000, I had a feeling that we were about to fall into a trap that would suck us deeper into an abysmal quagmire of debt. None of our families who have lost loved ones in Iraq have any peace to why they lost their family member because of a war that should never have even been considered a smart move.

Bush and Cheney have destroyed all that we had worked so hard to achieve. They stole all the surplus and ran away to hide. Problems are, they can't leave the country because The Hague has a warrant out for their arrest for committing war crimes. And we are just standing here scared to death not trying to prosecute these criminals in our country! WE have allowed them to speak out and be seen recently in the media, even after their destruction process had only contributed to their wealth. Mission accomplished. We are such idiots, and each one who does not vote in every election is to blame.

If you think that staying home and hoping that the taxes will increase on the wealthy, and this income will provide your family with more substance, you are sadly fooled again and again. The rich folks will always buy the politicians who create the laws that exclude them from having to participate in our taxation system. The same people are making sure that we pay the taxes, so they can continue to receive welfare cash for their large companies. Do we see a pattern here yet?

Perhaps the only way to our hearts ae through our wallets. I am very sad to see the population of our planet equate their individual values with a dollar amount. We have no other recourse except to speak up and say something for a change. Some of us are verbal and will create a dialogue which includes every facet of social position. And some will cower in a corner and complain that they are victims the ultimate oppressors in government. Well, apparently we are not aware of the barriers which have been installed to block our every move in politics. If we had any idea of the contrived voting process already in place, we might become more vocal in our needs as voters.

Chapter 31
Let's recap our new voting ideas

If we remember why we vote, half the confusion should lift from our foggy minds. At this point, we can understand that every election will have a measure or candidate who creates the environment for our life. So we should probably be more inquisitive in their motives, background, and past achievements before voting them into office.

Our friends at Forward Progressives summed up the quick an efficient way to piss off teabaggers or extreme right wing conservatism and their rhetoric. These are fun facts in which you can refer when more bullshit comes out of their mouths. I use this information from time to time to see if anyone screaming at me is paying attention, or the least bit current on events. Gosh, I can usually get someone to stop screwing with me after only one or two of these facts. Usually, sputtering and frustration emit when these factoids come forth. I try not to continue the bashing and choose to walk away with no more enabling of ignorance.

http://www.forwardprogressives.com/annoy-republicans/

- Nowhere in our Constitution does it say we're a Christian nation. In fact, nowhere in our Constitution does the word "Christian" appear even once.

- Freedom of religion also means freedom from religion—it also doesn't specify any particular religion.

- The 2nd Amendment actually refers to a "well-regulated militia." While it says the right for Americans to keep and bear arms shall not be infringed, the phrase "well regulated" obviously infers that this right doesn't come without regulations.

- Our Constitution doesn't mention anything about our nation having to be based on pure Capitalism.

- A corporation is an entity, not a person, and our Constitution wasn't created to protect the rights to entities—they have none.

- Education is more important than national defense. What's the point of a strong national defense if there's nothing worth defending?

- There are far more poor and middle-class Americans than rich

- If you continue building a society based on taking from the many to benefit the few, then we're not going to have a nation much longer.

- Rich people didn't become rich by giving away their money

- Trickle-down Economics is the biggest con our country has ever seen.

- Decades ago we all paid a much higher tax percentage, and our economic policies protected the people more than businesses. During these times, our nation saw historic growth and unheard of economic prosperity. None of that was done by basing our policies on giving more to the rich.

- Perhaps most news seems liberally biased because your news sources refuse to report facts.

- Being Muslim doesn't mean someone isn't American. Islam is a religion, not a nationality.

- George W. Bush actually did double our national debt; President Obama has not.

- Bush also inherited a balanced budget. It was his tax cuts and unfunded wars that sent us back into budget deficits.

- Social Security and Medicare is socialism— and millions of Republican voters benefit from, and receive, these benefits.

- Health insurance is you paying for another person's health care—in fact, all insurance is you paying for someone else.

- We had record oil prices under Bush, not Obama.

- The "Great Recession" started in 2008 while Obama took office January 20, 2009—you know, after the recession started.

- If Obama is the cause of our economic problems, why do Republicans avoid, at all costs, being associated with George W. Bush?

I understand that the discrepancy in the wording of our Constitution and how people could mistake a few small nuances in the legal form. I do not understand, however, that complete disregard for the content used as a "talking point" as their means of attention. How can the obvious sentences in this document be so ultimately cherry picked and torn to shreds?

We must remember to maintain all forms of logic and remain steadfast in our voting. We should probably plan ahead as to how to avoid any discussion regarding the "usual talking points" provided from a source. The usual need for leveling the playing field is not to overload the facts. People who are uneducated become violent instead of rational. Most have severe Anger Management issues and have never sought help. The last thing I need is someone who needs just one more thing to go wrong before they snap. I would like to remain the person who made them smile, instead.

I have backed down plenty of times when I realize that the alternate view is so far-fetched, the content could be a fantasy movie or cartoon. I am always surprised at the attention seeking scenarios the fear mongers come up with to try to scare people into submission. I am not easily fooled. Not like I used to be when I did not bother to find out facts instead of just accepting them as truth because I might have seen the story on TV.

Step easily in approaching folks who are already deep in discussion. Instead of throwing in cockeyed information at the inappropriate time, listening and getting a feel for the basis of the subject helps in political confidence.

Every time you think of voting the smile should cross your face and the ultimate knowledge that you have driven some oppressor into a small village of idiots by voting. I just squeal when I know that the person is bashing me the other day will have his or her vote canceled out when I walk into the booth. You see, rebellion remains obtained by understanding the power of voting will help to achieve a controlled and palatable environment for all to enjoy.

We have not embraced sharing yet in our country. We seem to keep going back to the exclusivity and judgments based on things that are totally irrelevant in 2015. Skin color is an exterior cover. That's all. WE ARE THE SAME under that pigment. There seems no logic in differentiating the societal imprint or generalization of someone based upon the "wrapping paper".

What kind of idiots are we? We accept all colors of dogs and cats and love them desperately, and unconditionally. We treat them like family and do not even give their coloration a second thought. But yet, another human (same species, you dumb asses) who is far different than you because of their "coat color" becomes an enemy?

This about the foolishness the people have created. All based upon control. Power and domination. The same goes for women. The power and control by the laws enacted are all executed by white males. What the heck is up with that? Like we can't even figure out if we close our eyes, the race factor does not exist. If we are blinded, we do not see the wrapping.

We are all consumers, and every piece of clothing and haircut has something to do with our packaging. All the cars we drive, the way we dress is about the visual. Somehow we have lost track of the basis for existence on the planet. We need air, water, and shelter first. The silly material items are precisely why we know money equals debt. Not love, compassion, nurturing, thriving, or happiness. Money has been an enormous reason for all things bad. I know you all will say, "and some good too" but if this is true, the fact that we have to deliver money to solve problems confuses the argument.

You see, the money is not the basis for all things that are truly free in the world. Yes, the water, the land, the air, animals and the plant life. Someone decided as time passed to divide this all up and try to hoard the resources to obtain more power over others.   Some greedy individual decided that the land was "theirs" and others would have to give something in return for occupancy.

The natives indigenous to the lands never made anyone pay for the use. They may have designated their tribal areas, but rarely did anyone try to overcome others because they had more. The value system is bullshit and our purpose for living sidestepped by those who would want to control the masses.

If we were to vote and attempt to use the democracy that was intended for us, we could head the planet to a recovery. If we were to spend a few hours learning a few things about the measures and issues up for a vote, we could have a better surrounding. Continuous stripping of resources could destroy the places we live and the geographic surrounding areas. I watched the fights and remembered reading about certain bills introduced which had the "add on" provisions eliminating the EPA to have jurisdiction on Fracking Companies. Dick Cheney had opened the floodgates allowing the penetration of the earth's crust by toxic chemicals to flow freely. All without the consequence of the violation of the environmental restrictions.

As I watched the <u>Gasland 2010</u> documentary, I then understood what was going on. My recall of the voting and measures I had read previously became a reality in the way fracking chemicals were seeping through to the water tables, flowing into the rivers, and destabilizing the ground area. Voting for office with multiple greedy people who would sell anything for a quick buck had taken over. The people affected were incapable of defending their property and right to live without toxins dumped on them. If a law is making sure a company does not kill people, animals, and resources have already been enacted, then how had the enforcement of this law certainly died? How was it possible to stand at a water faucet in one's home and set the dang thing on fire!?

Chapter 32
We vote to help other states as well

So the result in a few more documentaries, and the follow-up to Gasland 2010, I am finally beginning to understand how these things happen. The people of the area had put in place a very shady governing system who were in cahoots with the local drilling and oil companies. Pretty simple explanation. We then watched the laws change, become ignored, and simply disregarded as enforceable. Shameful, eh?

Now could someone tell me that the voters in Pennsylvania are any smarter or dumber than the rest of us? They are indeed not foolish, and the corruption in office for their State, County, and City officials all participated in the profits from the excess fracking. So the voting worked, but the enforcement of the laws did not. I am very aware of how many voters could have made a stink about the laws not obeyed were destroying the local area and resources.

So the valuable use of a vote was in vain? No. The common thread to these and many other issues squarely falls on the officials overseeing the state and its funding. Now, how can we better police the people who are taking bribes, pay-offs, or hush money to ignore the toxic demise of the natural resources? We are allowed to use these lakes, rivers, and water tables for our wells. We bought the property and presumed the neighbors would not be trying to kill us.

Our need to be a part of the general citizens' collection and try to make our cities safe persist as a constant. If your neighbor decides to start a moonshine still and it blows up, setting everything on fire, I will presume we could call the police. How do we call the authorities on a million dollar Oil Company who will be very glad to shoot you dead if confronted about such illegal activities?

Oh sure, I can see the call being placed right now, "Yeah, police?.. My water in my sink is catching on fire, and we are all being poisoned by the fracking company next door. We are all passing out and the water well has a 10-foot flame coming out of it." Of course the Police response would be, "Oh sorry, you need to call the fire department!"

We are only as powerful as we begin collectively gathered in common needs. Each person who has been violated by the oil companies has never had a chance to retaliate or receive any apologies. In any fashion. Sadly, the same companies are fracking the same areas, and people are beginning to move out instead of fighting.

So you ask, "What does Pennsylvania have to do with me? I live nowhere near that place". Well, the people of Pennsylvania were duped into believing their votes and the people representing them were going to follow the law. Oops. I suppose some part of that process had gone awry as the people involved have been caught red-handed pulling crap on the serious environment violations. And they do not care.

My point is that the people have not been paying attention to how the laws and rules are enforced. If the people had gathered together in a VERY large mass, the companies would have to back down. They would do so because they would be afraid to draw attention the thousands of over fracked wells failing, spilling into waterways, and toxifying the water tables. This fracking fallout has been spreading all over the country, and now Oklahoma is the number one for earthquakes brought forth by fracking.

The North and Southwest has started to see heavy fracking. These oil/gas companies and fracking companies' places intrude on the land where folks are buying ranches way out in the middle of nowhere. They are soon watching fracking wells pop up right next door to their property lines. Most will even start their wells on people's property and state that they have the mineral rights or some other jurisdiction crap.

We seem to be oblivious to the fact that we vote for laws that protect other states too. If my state's representative is fighting against fracking, the result of the fight assists other states. My vote, to put this person into office, has certainly helped to keep Pennsylvania's water clean, and the fracking companies thrown out. Also the coal industry in these states. I am fully aware that the states would like to eliminate coal. The leaders and owners of the mines are against removal and halting of coal use.

My vote helped to bring forth many wonderful laws and rights. My vote has put many people into office who have changed our world for the better. My vote has been used to stop the bad voter from taking money for his vote.

I think we just have a problem with having to execute the task of voting. Maybe it's the time element and the dragging yourself out to the polling place to do the deed or maybe the fact that the reasons for voting seem hard to comprehend. No matter ow you look at it, the voters are just not there anymore. So we should have the ballot include American Idol voting as well as Congress and President? Or maybe voting for the candidates available is like picking a mosquito out of a swarm. Choosing the bullet that you want to be shot in the head with? I can think of many similarities.

So thinking about the process makes us all frustrated, bored, and complacent. I understand. But not to vote is the same as watching the rest of the civilized world proceed in killing, raping, robbing, and terrorizing us all, and just pulling down the shade. We need help to be able to change the way this world has developed. We need people who have a brain to think critically and choose better leaders. But most of all, we need to vote.

I know that my vote for President will help the rest of the country, and by voting my State's senator and representative, the person showing up in Washington DC will truly fight for the whole country's rights and laws. If we have seen the graph as to which states have problems with moving forward, just take the Civil War map, draw the Mason-Dixon Line and notice the similarities. Are truly that stupid? Why are we not just calling these states out and telling them to stop. Oh, by the way, I do not need to reside in another state to call them on their civil rights violations, terror activities, and racist violence towards others. Last I looked, I could move about the whole country without having to have a passport to get into the other states. And the House is trying to allow the states to declare their borders un-crossable for refugees? Borders of our states are for taxation purposes only. A state cannot put a guard at the border and keep people out.

I want to participate in all the states activities, and help other people understand how much their vote affects the rest of the USA. I also think that the new trend of Voting Parties will take hold because the younger folks are far more social, and the aspect of coming together to learn as well as have a great time appears as their everyday and normal way of life. So why not capitalize on the fun and excitement so as to create joy and gratification from casting a vote.

To start up the Voting Party idea, I will be publishing a "kit" which will have everything needed to make the "serious part of voting without excess crap to drag to the party. I will provide games, and visual stimulation in DVD format. If I have the proper pamphlets, sample ballots, and all the food and drink, you can consume, the party will have started! Hopefully, a few games thrown in will keep the party moving, and some jokes as well as music to keep the flow.

Inviting friends will be pretty simple. If there are people with conflicting views or party affiliations, prepare to remind them at the entrance of the party that no bickering is allowed. Only facts and sources will be allowed to these parties. Nobody who is in the judgement of others and the way they party will be allowed either. If there is a objection about the booze or weed at the party, then they must go. Toleration is only allowed. Negativity will not be included in the process. If a person chooses to vote differently, then so be it. The act of the party is to understand the issues better. The purpose is to help people choose wisely and with the correct information. The material used will be unbiased and informative.

I am a true believer of comfort and wisdom going hand in hand. The ease of which to be able to choose and decipher information when voting comes with practice. The thrill still comes with the act, itself. And of course, the fun starts with the Voting Party, and then the Celebration party afterward! And we can all cry in our beers if we lose, but at least we will console ourselves, together.

Chapter 33
The Party starts now

So we have finally come to the part where the party starts, the first cocktail has started to take effect, and we are going to do this voting thing together! Now, I will hand out this booklet I have devised, and a pen for everyone who is a registered voter. I will do everything I can to help you feel comfortable about doing the voting thing and walk away with a new confidence in participation. I can make sure the topics are made to suit a normal level of intelligence, while creating ways to help you have a fun conversation, eat, and enjoy the company.

I will advise choosing the people to invite by asking them first if they are interested in doing something different this time when they prepare to vote. Most folks would be pretty keen on a party that a voting theme would be the basis.   I can imagine many of my friends who would love a gathering of "like minded" people in a goofy night of gathering data and preparing to vote.

Try not to invite folks who are more apt to create conflict amongst the rest of the party goers. I know they may want to participate, but there are rules before coming to this event, and everyone must agree before arriving.   If there are any conflicts, the dynamics of the flow will easily be curtailed by those who are not combative. Most people I know are very easy to talk to and understand a great deal about basic common sense. Also, I am certain that people are not foolish to have created a negative environment for the others. Even having too many beers can make the nicest person quite angry or combative. The ambiance of a party is fun, music, people, and grog.

If we start something strange like a Political Voting Bash or maybe an All-Night Voter's Rave, I would be there in a heartbeat. What a blast to use the ambiance and feelings of happiness drive my interest to make a mark by voting. I know this idea seems a little nutty, but I am thinking more along the lines of trying to liven up this very solemn duty. The way people deal with voting nowadays is just pathetic. Most people haven't voted in years. Many still feel that the voting doesn't work and no matter who they vote for, the disappointment ensues.

I think at if you have gone as far as to take an interest in making a statement and supporting like-minded ideas, then voting is certainly a way to extend that desire with some concrete gratification. If we could only take a few minutes to check out the rebellion factor, we could be our little group of radicals! I can be radical about food and how we eat, or I can be an activist for clean air and water. We are all having to rebel at some point, and about numerous things that piss us off. Why don't we just extend the same fight to help others and make our surroundings better for everyone?

Coexist. That's all we want. Most of the people in our world who are angry and helpless to understand their predicament will always come out fighting. So why shouldn't we? Is there a force that frightens us to a point of cowering in a corner and covering our ears? We haven't got much time left if we want to make the world a better place. We have been warned, and yet the same people keep arriving on Capitol Hill and their career politics function as usual. Well, I for one am not ready to give up the many rights we have been fighting for this many years. And I will continue to vote, while trying to urge others to play reindeer games too!

If we all get together a few times a year to find out different views and discover new thoughts we have then been on this earth to participate. I do believe that the many people who have problems discerning the facts from the fantasy have been sucked into a vacuum of negative, fear invoking, and death threats. I have been watching the fearful for a long time, and I know there are better ways to achieve comfort in democracy.

I believe in my country and the ideas that came forth when we were new. I also think that the idea of self-governing is an outstanding concept. We created the Constitution so as to be able to change the laws as time went on. The founding fathers had planned on the needs of the future generations. We just have a few problems with those who would not be satisfied with a large amount of "stuff", so we need to teach them to share. We also need to teach those who have only one thought in their minds. Money. I do believe the priorities around here are totally screwed up, and survival is based upon how much money is possessed by humans.

Sheesh people. Really? Money? The next time you look into your child's eyes, or see the most beautiful sky remember how much it cost you at that moment to feel exhilaration. This pleasure will cost you nothing. But if we allow the greedy to suck our resources to from underneath our feet, we will never see the wonderful natural beauty, for free. Nor will we be able to pass the same beauty along to future generations.

We will keep voting, and hoping that we will hit the jackpot on the masses coming together to make the planet safe, healthy, and a total party for the humans that reside here!

Rock on, party on and vote, please?